The Complete Learn Spanish For Adult

Beginners Book (3 in 1)

Master Reading, Writing, and Speaking Spanish With This Simple 3 Step Process

Worldwide Nomad

FREE GIFT

Inside this gift you'll find:

Online Pronunciation Course: Easily perfect pronunciation through an online video course for audio learners

TO CLAIM BONUS

Scan the QR Code below

OR

Visit the link below:

https://worldwidenomadbooks.com/Spanish-free-course

Index

Spanish Phrasebook For Beginners

Spanish Grammar Workbook and Textbook For *Beginners*

Learn Spanish With Essential, Easy to Understand Lessons

Worldwide Nomad

Introduction

Throughout history, there have been different manifestations and expressions based on some form of Spanish. The Spanish language has its variances, which mainly depend on the country in which it is being spoken, as well as the era.

There have been many learning methods throughout time - some are professionally designed while others are more organic, such as a child who grows up speaking Spanish as their native language or a non-Spanish speaker who moves to a country where Spanish is the common language.

There are several variations of Spanish spoken in Latin America. Some countries are more influenced by European Spanish while others are based more on regional/dialectical influences.

The Spanish language, like others, has a wide range of grammatical elements, and each of the structures contained therein are of great importance. Nouns have two genders (masculine and feminine), simple and compound tenses, words similar to others belonging to other languages (although sometimes they mean the opposite), and two different modes of expression (indicative and subjunctive). All of this leads to the knowledge of a language that, although complex, is very rich and spoken around the world. The intention of this work is to help the reader or student have a solid foundation when learning this language.

What is the indicative mood in Spanish?

The indicative mood of sentences in Spanish refers to actions that occur in any verb tense and are expressed in a real and everyday way. That is, there are no hypotheses, desires, probabilities or doubts that said actions will occur. For any native person of any Spanish-speaking country, it is normal to express themselves in this way. Still, this one tends to be easy for people learning Spanish. Within the complement of sentences in this mode of expression, there are small words called *prepositions*, which will be explained in each section of this book. They help link words and verbs in order to give each sentence a coherent meaning in relation to other people included in said sentences, places and times.

In this book, you will find all information about the indicative mode. In Spanish, there are two modes; the indicative and the subjunctive (which includes probabilities, doubts, and other forms of expressions).

Affirmative sentence structure (indicative mode).

The structure to form affirmative sentences in Spanish, the indicative mode is as follows:

In most cases, these begin with the subject who performs them. This can be made up of a person, group of people, objects, situations, places, frequency with which an activity is carried out, demonstrative pronouns, or even personal pronouns. The subject is normally followed by a verb or action, and then a complement, which can at the same time be composed of various words that will become known throughout the reading of this book.

The Spanish language varies according to the country where it is spoken and the region within each country. Both its pronunciation and the great variety of words with the same meaning and different expressions make learning Spanish a wonderfully interesting experience.

A person acquires speaking and pronunciation skills from early childhood on- When learning a language, it is necessary for the student to reinforce the meaning and order of each grammatical structure on a daily basis, and to also place great emphasis on pronunciation. Such is the case with the letter "r" in Spanish, as well as other languages. It is a letter to which greater attention must be paid in order to achieve a type of expression that demonstrates clarity and excellence.

As expressed previously, it is of great value to know the different nuances or meanings that some words have. In Spanish there is so much linguistic richness that the same word can have different meanings.

Furthermore, depending on the verb tense, the conjugation of irregular verbs does not vary. There are different conjugation structures of the verb, which must be studied and put into practice progressively. This will help make your learning experience a great one.

The Spanish alphabet is the same as English, except for some letters.

To complete each expression in Spanish, each complement varies depending on elements such as: place, more people within the grammatical expression or sentence, days, dates, frequency in which the action occurs, and the type of expression; if it is a sentence of common expression or of expressing advice, opinions, mandate, etc.

Chapter 1

1.1 Alphabet

The alphabet in Spanish is the same as in English. There are a few more words, but, in general, it is the same.

Observe the alphabet

	Sounds in Spanish
a	a
b	be
c	se
d	de
e	e
f	efe
g	ge
h	ache
i	ee
j	jota
k	ca
l	ele
m	eme
n	ene
ñ	eñe
o	o
p	pe
q	cu
r	ere
s	ese
t	te
u	u
v	ve
w	dobleve
x	equis
y	y
z	zeta

1.2 Days of the week

The days of the week in Spanish are as follows:

domingo	Sunday
lunes	Monday
martes	Tuesday
miércoles	Wednesday
jueves	Thursday
viernes	Friday
sábado	Saturday

1.3 Cardinal numbers

Cardinal numbers are those that have a very general use. In most cases they refer to quantities of objects that someone possesses, observes, desires, or exist in an everyday environment. In Spanish, they are the following:

1 uno	1 one
2 dos	2 two
3 tres	3 three
4 cuatro	4 four
5 cinco	5 five
6 seis	6 six
7 siete	7 seven
8 ocho	8 eight
9 nueve	9 nine
10 diez	10 ten
11 once	11 eleven
12 doce	12 twelve
13 trece	13 thirteen
14 catorce	14 fourteen
15 quince	15 quince
16 dieciséis	16 sixteen
17 diecisiete	17 seventeen

18 dieciocho	18 eighteen
19 diecinueve	19 nineteen
20 veinte	20 twenty

21 veintiuno	21 twenty one
22 veintidós	22 twenty two
23 veintitres	23 twenty thrcc
24 veinticuatro	24 twenty four
25 veinticinco	25 twenty five
26 veintiséis	26 twenty six
27 veintisiete	27 twenty seven
28 veintiocho	28 twenty eight
29 veintinueve	29 twenty nine
30 treinta	30 thirty

31 treinta y uno	31 thirty one
32 treinta y dos	32 thirty two
33 treinta y tres	33 thirty three
34 treinta y cuatro	34 thirty four
35 treinta y cinco	35 thirty five
36 treinta y seis	36 thirty six
37 treinta y seis	37 thirty six
38 treinta y ocho	38 thirty eight
39 treinta y nueve	39 thirty nine
40 cuarenta	40 forty

41 cuarenta y uno	41 forty one
42 cuarenta y dos	42 forty two
43 cuarenta y tres	43 forty three
44 cuarenta y cuatro	44 forty four
45 cuarenta y cinco	45 forty five
46 cuarenta y seis	46 forty six
47 cuarenta y siete	47 forty seven

48 cuarenta y ocho	48 forty eight
49 cuarenta y nueve	49 forty nine
50 cincuenta	50 fifty

51 cincuenta y uno	51 fifty one
52 cincuenta y dos	52 fifty two
53 cincuenta y tres	53 fifty three
54 cincuenta y cuatro	54 fifty four
55 cincuenta y cinco	55 fifty five
56 cincuenta y seis	56 fifty six
57 cincuenta y siete	57 fifty seven
58 cincuenta y ocho	58 fifty eight
59 cincuenta y nueve	59 fifty nine
60 sesenta	60 sixty

61 sesenta y uno	61 sixty one
62 sesenta y dos	62 sixty two
63 sesenta y tres	63 sixty three
64 sesenta y cuatro	64 sixty four
65 sesenta y cinco	65 sixty five
66 sesenta y seis	66 sixty six
67 sesenta y siete	67 sixty seven
68 sesenta y ocho	68 sixty eight
69 sesenta y nueve	69 sixty nine
70 setenta	70 seventy

71 setenta y uno	71 seventy one
72 setenta y dos	72 seventy two
73 setenta y tres	73 seventy three
74 setenta y cuatro	74 seventy four
75 setenta y cinco	75 seventy five
76 setenta y seis	76 seventy six
77 setenta y siete	77 seventy seven

78 setenta y ocho	78 seventy eight
79 setenta y nueve	79 seventy nine
80 ochenta	80 eighty

81 ochenta y uno	81 eighty one
82 ochenta y dos	82 eighty two
83 ochenta y tres	83 eighty three
84 ochenta y cuatro	84 eighty four
85 ochenta y cinco	85 eighty five
86 ochenta y seis	86 eighty six
87 ochenta y siete	87 eighty seven
88 ochenta y ocho	88 eighty eight
89 ochenta y nueve	89 eighty nine
90 noventa	90 ninety

91 noventa y uno	91 ninety one
92 noventa y dos	92 ninety two
93 noventa y tres	93 ninety three
94 noventa y cuatro	94 ninety four
95 noventa y cinco	95 ninety five
96 noventa y seis	96 ninety-six
97 noventa y siete	97 ninety-seven
98 noventa y ocho	98 ninety-eight
99 noventa y nueve	99 ninety-nine
100 cien	100 hundred

Starting from 101, the way numbers are written is different.

101 ciento uno	101 hundred one
102 ciento dos	102 one hundred two
103 ciento tres	103 one hundred three
104 ciento cuatro	104 one hundred four
105 ciento cinco	105 one hundred five
106 ciento seis	106 one hundred six

107 ciento siete	107 one hundred seven
108 ciento ocho	108 one hundred eight
109 ciento nueve	109 one hundred nine
110 ciento diez	110 one hundred ten

Then all the other numbers remain in the same way as their base forms.

Starting with the second hundred, the numbers are written as follows:

200 doscientos	200 two hundred
300 trescientos	300 three hundred
400 cuatrocientos	400 four hundred
500 quinientos	500 five hundred
600 seiscientos	600 six hundred
700 setecientos	700 seven hundred
800 ochocientos	800 eight hundred
900 novecientos	900 nine hundred
1000 mil	1000 thousand

10.000 diez mil	10,000 ten thousand
100.000 cien mil	100,000 one hundred thousand
1.000.000 un millón	1,000,000 one million

1.4 Countable and uncountable nouns

Before practicing, it is important to know the difference between ¿cuánto? (how much? / for uncountable / masculine nouns), ¿cuánta? (for uncountable / feminine nouns)¿cuántos? (how many?/ for countable, masculine nouns) and ¿cuántas (how many? / for countable, feminine nouns)

Observe the following interrogative sentences; with countable and uncountable nouns.

Tiempo: Uncountable noun	¿Cuánto tiempo?	How much time?
Agua: uncountable noun	¿Cuánta agua?	How much water?
Años: countable noun	¿Cuántos años?	How many years?
Flores: countable noun	¿Cuántas flores?	How many flowers?

Observe the following vocabulary (countable and countable nouns).

Palabras contables	Countable nouns
casa	house
carro	car
libro	book
cuaderno	notebook
computadora	computer
mesa	table

Observe the following vocabulary (uncountable nouns)

tiempo	time
energía	energy
leche	milk
agua	water
sal	salt
azúcar	sugar

1.5 Verb "haber"

Normally, the verb "haber", which means "there is"/ "there are" is used in these types of sentences.

hay	There is (singular)
hay	There is (plural)

To make questions, the right form is as follows:

¿Cuántos libros hay en el estante?	How many books are there on the shelf?	Libros: countable noun
¿Cuánta agua hay en el refrigerador?	How much water is there in the refrigerator?	Agua: uncountable noun

The answer for countable nouns questions should be based in numbers;

¿Cuántos libros hay en el estante?	How many books are there on the shelf?
Hay 10	There are 10

¿Cuántos juguetes hay en el estante de los niños?	How many toys are there on the kid's shelf?
Hay 25 juguetes	There are 25 toys

¿Cuántos carros hay en el estacionamiento?	How many cars are there in the garage?
Hay 30 carros	There are 30 cars

¿Cuántos animales hay en el zoológico?	How many animals are there in the zoo?
Hay muchos / Hay muchos animales en el zoológico	There are many / There are many animals at the zoo

¿Cuántos platos hay en la mesa?	How many plates are there on the table?
Hay 8 platos	There are 8 plates

1.6 Verb "tener"

Observe an example with the verb "tener" (to have) conjugated.

¿Cuántos pares de zapatos tienes?	How many pairs of shoes do you have?
Tengo 8 pares de zapatos	I have 8 pairs of shoes

*Remember in Spanish, verbs are sometimes used directly conjugated; not necessarily with a subject or subject pronoun.

Observe how the verb "tener" is conjugated.

Yo tengo	I have
Tú tienes	You have
Él tiene	He has
Ella tiene	She has
Usted tiene	You have
Nosotros tenemos	We have (masculine/feminine, masculine)
Nosotras tenemos	We have
Ustedes tienen	You have (masculine/feminine, masculine)
Ellos tienen	They have (masculine/feminine, masculine)
Ellas tienen	They have (female)

Observe the following conversation.

Patricia and Luis are for the first time in a city. They are really surprised with the new sights.

Patricia:	Luis, ¡mira cuántos edificios hay!	Luis, look how many buildings there are!
Luis:	Sí, Patricia; ¡hay muchos, y muy grandes!	Yes, Patricia; there are many, and really big!
Patricia:	¿Alrededor de cuántos hay en tu ciudad?	Around how many are there in your city?
Luis:	En realidad, no sé. Probablemente 100 de este tipo	I really don't know. Probably 100 of this type.
Patricia:	Muchos	A lot.
Luis:	En realidad, hay muchas casas	Really, there are many houses.
Patricia:	¡Genial!	Great!

Practice

1.- Write and spell your name in Spanish.

_____

2.- Write and spell your lastname in Spanish.

_____

3.-Arrange the following words to make a question and answer.

_____

hoy?	día	¿Qué	es
es	miércoles	Hoy	

4.- From the following sentences, underline the countable nouns.

En el mar hay muchos peces	There are many fish in the sea
Carlos trabaja por muchas horas	Carlos works for many hours
¿Tienes algún lápiz?	Do you have any pencil?
Pablo limpia todas las mesas en el restaurante	Pablo cleans all the tables at the restaurant
Carolina y Beatriz hablan con los niños	Carolina and Beatriz talk with the kids

Chapter 2

2.1 Ordinal numbers

Ordinal numbers are those that place any noun (singular and plural) within a place, either tangibly or intangible. They have gender; (masculine or feminine), and quantity (singular and plural). These are:

1 º primero, primera	1st first
2º segundo, segunda	2nd second
3º tercero, tercera	3rd third
4º cuarto, cuarta	4th fourth
5º quinto, quinta	5th fifth
6º sexto, sexta	6th sixth
7º séptimo, séptima	7th seventh
8º octavo, octava	8th eighth
9º noveno, novena	9th ninth
10º décimo, décima	10th tenth

11º décimo primero / undécimo	11th eleventh
12º décimo segundo / duodécimo	12th twelfth
13º décimo tercero	13th thirteenth
14º décimo cuarto	14th fourteenth
15º décimo quinto	15th fifteenth
16º décimo sexto	16th sixteenth
17º décimo séptimo	17th seventeenth
18º décimo octavo	18th eighteenth
19º décimo noveno	19th nineteenth
20º vigésimo	20th twentieth

21º vigésimo primero	21st twenty-first
22º vigésimo segundo	22nd twenty-second
23º vigésimo tercero	23rd twenty-third
24º vigésimo cuarto	24th twenty-fourth
25º vigésimo quinto	25th twenty-fifth
26º vigésimo sexto	26th twenty-sixth

27° vigésimo séptimo	27th twenty-seventh
28° vigésimo octavo	28th twenty-eighth
29° vigésimo noveno	29th twenty-ninth

30° trigésimo	30th thirtieth
40° cuadragésimo	40th fortieth
50° quincuagésimo	50th fiftieth
60° sexagésimo	60th sixtieth
70° septuagésimo	70th seventieth
80° octogésimo	80° eighty
90° nonagésimo	90th ninetieth
100° centésimo	100th hundredth

All of the above numbers are gendered; masculine and feminine.

Look at some examples:

Carlos es el segundo hijo	Carlos is the second son
Es la primera vez que visito ese lugar	It's the first time I visit that place
Él obtuvo el tercer lugar en la competencia	He took third place in the competition.
Ellos viven en el cuarto piso	They live on the fourth floor
Pablo no visitó la ciudad por segunda vez	Paul did not visit the city a second time
¿Fuiste al parque por tercera vez?	Did you go to the park for the third time?

Although the grammatical explanation of the sentences above will be seen in the next lessons, it is advisable to understand the use of ordinal numbers in context.

2.2 Family

Names of family members are as follows:

bisabuela	great-grandmother
bisabuelo	great-grandfather
abuelo	grandfather
abuela	grandmother

padre / papá	father
madre / mamá	mother
padres	parents
hija	daughter
hijo	son
hijos	children
tío	uncle
tía	aunt
primo	cousin
prima	cousin

In expressions referring to family members, it is used the verb "to be" as "ser" (conjugated) plus a possessive pronun (will be studied in following lessons).

Examples:

Carolina es tu mamá	Carolina is your mother
Verónica es mi hermana	Veronica is my sister
Carlos es mi abuelo	Carlos is my grandfather

2.3 Telling the time

In Spanish, there are different forms to tell the time. For so, the type of numbers used is the cardinal ones. According to the occasion, the way to ask is expressed.

When asking the time, the definite pronoun used is "la" for singular, which is 1:00 am/pm + minutes. For plural forms, the definitive pronouns is "las"+ time am/pm.

Type of questions #1:

a) ¿Qué hora es?	What time is it?
b) Son las 10:00 en punto	It's 10:00 o'clock

To ask about an event:

a) ¿A qué hora es el concierto?	What time is the concert?
b) A las 3:30 pm	A las 3:30 pm

To ask politely:

a) ¿Me podría, por favor, decir la hora?	Could you please, tell me the time?
b) ¡Seguro! Son las 2: 45 pm	Sure! It is 2:45 pm

Look at the conversation about the time.

a) Hola, ¿cómo estás? ¿Me podrías, por favor decir la hora?	Hi, how are you? Could you please, tell me the time?
b) Hola, muy bien, ¿y tú? Seguro!	b) Hi, very well, and you? Sure!

Expressions to refer to time. To add the amount of minutes after the expressed time, the expressions in Spanish are:

Es la 1 + y + minutos	It's 1 + and + minutes

For plural forms the expressions are these types:

Son las 2 + y + minutos	It's 2 + and + minutes
Son las 5 + y + minutos	It's 5 + y + minutes

Normally, when the way to tell the time expressing the minutes before reaching to the following one, expressions are:

Veinte para las tres	Twenty to three
Un cuarto para las cuatro	A quarter to four
Diez para las seis	Ten to six
Cinco para las cuatro	Five to four

But, sometimes, the expression "falta" or "faltan" is used to mean the missing minutes to reach to the next time.

¿Qué hora es?	What time is it?
Faltan veinte para las doce	It's twenty to twelve

¿Qué hora es?	What time is it?
Faltan cinco para las diez	It's five to ten

Observe some expressions based on above ones; ¿A qué hora + verb/complement? To ask about the time an event usually occurs.

¿A qué hora vas a la escuela?	What time do you go to school?
¿A qué hora desayunas con tu familia?	What time do you have breakfast with your family?
¿A qué hora estudias?	What time do you study?
¿A qué hora almuerzas?	What time do you have lunch?
¿A qué hora cenas?	What time do you have dinner?

The above expressions can also be used with other subjects: tú (used in the previous expressions), él, ella, usted, nosotros, nosotras, ustedes, ellos, ellas.

Practice

Fill in the spaces with an ordinal number. Remember ordinal numbers take gender.

Estoy en el _____piso	I am on the _____floor
Carlos obtuvo el _____lugar	Carlos got the ____ place
Manuel es el _____ hijo	Manuel is the _____son

Complete the sentences with the appropiate information about family.

_____ es mi papá	_____ is my father
_____ es mi tía	_____ is my aunt
_____ es mi abuelo	_____ es mi grandfather
_____es mi primo	_____ is my cousin

Mark with an "x" (in the Spanish box) the appropite answer

Benjamín es mi tío_____ abuela_____	Benjamin is my uncle_____ grandmother_____
Luisa es mi papá_____ hermana_____	Luisa is my father_____ sister_____
Ellos son hermanos_____ papá_____	They are brothers_____ father

Complete the sentences with the appropiate form of the verb "ser" related to time.

¿Qué hora _____?	What time _____ it?
_____ la 1:00 en punto	_____ 1:00 o' clock
¿A qué hora _____ el evento?	What time _____ the event?
_____ a las 10:30 de la mañana	_____ at 10: 00 in the morning

Mark with a "x" the correct answer

Es las 2:00 pm en punto	It's 2:00 o'clock	
Son las 2:00 pm en punto		

Faltan 20 para las 3:00 pm	It's 20 to 3:00 pm	
Faltan las 20 para las 3:00 pm		

Mark with an "x" the correct expression

¿Qué hora es?	What time is it?	
¿Cuáles hora es?		

Chapter 3

3.1 Vocabulary related to parts of the house

casa	house
techo (inside)	ceiling
tejado	roof
cocina	kitchen
habitación	bedroom
sala	living room
comedor	dining room
baño	bathroom
pasillo	hall
escaleras	stairs
jardín	garden
garage	garage
ventana	window
cortina	curtain
puerta	door
alfombra	carpet
lámpara	lamp
mesa	table
silla	chair

Kitchen appliances / cookware:

estufa	stove
refrigerador	refrigerator
lavaplatos	dishwasher
plato	plate
vaso	glass / cup
cubertería	silverware
tenedor	fork
cuchillo	knife
cuchara	spoon

taza	cup
jarra	jug
servilletas	napkins
mantel	tablecloth
olla	pot
abrelatas	can opener
cafetera	coffee maker
horno microondas	microwave oven
horno	oven
gabinetes	cabinets
florero	vase

3.2 Vocabulary related to animals

araña	spider
águila	eagle
cerdo	pig
pollo	chicken
oveja	sheep
caballo	horse
gato	cat
perro	dog
elefante	elephant
león	lion
conejo	rabbit
ratón	mouse

Look, more specifically, at a different scenario in which animal vocabulary is included:

Zoo: some of the animals in Spanish are:

mono	mono
zebra	zebra

elefante	elephant
jirafa	giraffe
hipopótamo	hipoppotamus
camello	camel
aves	birds
serpientes	snakes
pez	fish
tortuga	tortoise
león	lion
tigre	tigre

In most cases, sentences expressing surprise or related to amazement at the appearance and size of the animals are used. In Spanish, they are:

¡Mira! ¡Qué jirafa tan grande!	Look! What a big giraffe!
¡Güau!, ¡qué bonitas aves!	Wow!, how beautiful birds!
¡Me dan miedo esas serpientes!	Those snakes scare me!
¡Cuidado!, ¡no te acerques al lago!	Be careful, don't go near the lake!
¿Puedo tomar una foto de los animales?	Can I take a photo of the animals?

3.3 Vocabulary related to airports

In relation to airports, it is possible to observe a lot of vocabulary similar to that used in English. There is vocabulary to express yourself about the counter, such as:

counter de la aerolínea	airline counter
avión	plane
pasaporte	passport
pase de abordaje	boarding pass
ticket	ticket
maletas	suitcases
pasajero	passenger
viajero	traveler
aerolínea	airline
aeropuerto	airport

puerta de embarque	boarding gate

There are also expressions likc:

¿Puedo ver su pasaporte?	Can I see your passport?
Sí, aquí está	Yes, is here
¿Cuántas personas viajan?	How many people are traveling?
¿Hacia dónde se dirige?	Where are you traveling?
Su puerta de embarque es la número (xx)	Your boarding gate is number (xx)
Puede colocar su equipaje por acá	You can put your luggage here
Aquí están las etiquetas para el equipaje	Here are the luggage tags

3.4 Vocabulary related to vacations

In relation to holidays, not all Spanish-speaking countries have the same seasons of the year; some have only two. This causes travelers to always use their own vocabulary for each season in some continents of the world. It also happens that schedules vary depending on the traveler's origin and destination location.

Other elements that must be taken into account when learning new vocabulary in different languages are those related to the type of travel and transportation, such as ferries, planes, buses, cars, cruises and trains.

3.5 Vocabulary related to types of transport

autobús	bus
avión	plane
tren	train
ferry	ferry
barco	ship
crucero	cruise
helicóptero	helicopter
moto	moto

In relation to the stations where each type of transport is taken (other than airports, they are observed)

estación de autobús	bus station
estación de tren	train station
puerto de ferry	ferry port
puerto de barco (o solo puerto marítimo)	ship port (or just sea port)
puerto aéreo (helicópteros)	air port (helicopters)

Observe expressions related to bus station:

La próxima salida hacia es destino es a las (time)	The next departure to this destination is at (time)
a)Perdón, ¿cuánto cuesta el ticket hacia (destino)? b) Cuesta (xxx)	a)Excuse me, how much does the ticket cost to (destination)? b) It costs (xxx)
¿LLeva usted equipaje?	Do you carry luggage?
¿Viajan menores de edad con usted?	Are minors traveling with you?

Observe the type of conversation with train stations.

¿Por dónde está la entrada a la estación del tren?	Where is the entrance to the train station?
La estación del tren está a dos cuadras	The train station is two blocks away
¿A qué hora sale el próximo tren?	What time does the next train leave?

Notice the kind of talk about seaports.

a)¿Dónde puedo adquirir los boletos hacia (destination)? b)Los puede adquirir en esa casilla c) ¡Muchas gracias!	a)Where can I purchase tickets to (destination) b)You can purchase them in that box c) Thank you very much!

Regarding helicopter ports, they normally offer rides, not long trips.

3.6 Vocabulary related to tours

When talking about tours, there is a large amount of vocabulary, depending on the tourist destination to which the traveler is going. Among them; beach, mountain, sports, history tours, among others, stand out.

Observe the vocabulary related to beach tours:

agencia de viajes	travel agency
agente de viajes	travel agent
reservación	reservation
número de viajeros	number of travelers
hotel	hotel
cabañas	cabins
playa	playa
disponibilidad	availability
ida solamente	one way only
ida y vuelta	round trip
paquetes turísticos	tourist packages

Observe a conversation related to this type of tours.

En la agencia de viajes…	In the travel agency…
a)Buenos días / buenas tardes ¿En qué le podemos ayudar?	a)Good morning / good afternoon, how can we help you?
b) ¡Hola!, buenos días. Me gustaría conocer los destinos de playa.	b) Hello! Good morning. I would like to know the beach destinations.
a)Sí, ¡claro! ¿a dónde le gustaría viajar?	a)Oh, yeah, sure! where would you like to travel?
b)Me gustaría conocer los destinos de playa de América del Sur	b)I would like to know the beach destinations in South America
a)¡Por supuesto! pase por aquí, ¡por favor! ¿Su viaje será ida y vuelta, o solo ida?	a)Of course! stop by, please! Will your trip be round trip, or just one way?
b)No, ida y vuelta.	b)No, round trip.

a)¡Seguro! Ofrecemos diferentes paquetes turísticos de ese tipo.	a) Sure! We offer different tourist packages of this type.
b) ¡Gracias!	b)Thank you!

Practice.

Underline the correct word for each option.

It is the place where someone lives: casa/lámpara/alfombra
External area of a house where plants are: cocina/jardín/sala
Place where you can stand and watch to the outside: puerta/cocina/ventana
Part of the house where family can cook / prepare meals: jardín/sala/cocina
Something standing or on a side table you can turn on/off: mesa/lámpara/ventana

Choose the correct word to give sense to the sentences

Puedes prender la Lámpara_____ Ventana_____	You can turn on the Lamp_____ Window_____
Elisa sube por la Escalera_____ Jardín_____	Elisa goes up the Stairs_____ Garden_____

Mark with an "x" the correct answer

Animal de color gris; muy grande Jirafa____ Elefante_____	Grey animal, very big Giraffe____ Elephant_____
Vive en el mar Pez_____ León_____	It lives in the sea Fish____ Lion_____

Mark with an "x" the correct answer

Tengo un pequeño Perro_____ Serpiente_____	I have a small Dog_____ Snake_____

Choose the correct word to complete the sentences about transport.

Puedes tomar un _____en la estación de trenes. Avión/ auto/ tren	You can take a _____at the train station. Plane/car/train
Puedes viajar por aire en_____a otros países. Barco/avión/auto	You can air travel to other countries by_____ Ship/plane/car
Carolina siempre va a la oficina en_____ Barco/auto/avión	Carolina always goes to the office by_____ Ship/car/plane

Mark with an "x" the correct answer

Siempre tomo el tren en la Aeropuerto_____ Estación de tren_____	I always take the bus at the Airport_____ Train station_____
Ella espera el bus en la Parada de bus____ Aeropuerto_____	She waits for the bus at the Bus stop_____ Airport_____

Chapter 4

4.1 Articles

In Spanish there are different types of articles; determined and indeterminate.

Certain articles are used to refer to specific nouns. For example, "the house" (la casa), where it is observed that "casa" is a feminine noun; Therefore, "la" is the definite article that corresponds to it. Observe the following table of certain articles.

article	singular/plural	male / female
el	singular	masculine
la	singular	female
los	plural	It can be a mix of masculine and feminine within a group. It can also refer to a group of masculine nouns
las	plural	female

Example:

la casa	home
la hoja	the sheet
la hora	the time
la cocina	the kitchen
la comida	food
la ensalada	salad
la sopa	soup
la mesa	table
la servilleta	napkin
la escuela	the school
la clase	class
la carpeta	folder
el libro	the book
el ferrocarril	the train
el bus	the bus
el helicóptero	the helicopter
el avión	the plane

los libros	the books
los ferrocarriles	the railways
los buses	los buses
los helicópteros	the helicopters
los aviones	the airplanes
el pez	the fish
el perro	the dog
el elefante	elephant
el gato	the cat
el cocodrilo	the crocodile
los animales	animals
los peces	fish
los perros	dogs
los gatos	the cats
los elefantes	the elephants
las casas	houses
las mesas	the tables
las calles	streets
las avenidas	avenues
las nacionalidades	the nationalities
las escuelas	the schools
las carpetas	the folders
las pizarras	the blackboards

Indefinite articles are those that refer to non-specific nouns, as their name suggests.

artículo	article	singular / plural	male Female
un	a / an	singular	masculine
una	a / an	singular	female
unos	some	plural	It can refer to a group of masculine and feminine nouns or to a group of masculine nouns only.
unas	some	plural	refers to a group of nouns of the feminine gender only.

4.2 Formation of plurals of nouns

In Spanish, plurals are formed by adding ""s" or "es".

Notice the singular and plural forms of some nouns.

singular	plural	singular	plural
casa	casas	house	houses
puerta	puertas	door	doors
ventana	ventanas	window	windows
lámpara	lámparas	lamp	lamps
alfombra	alfombras	rug	rugs
cocina	cocinas	kitchen	kitchens
mesa	mesas	mesa	tables
silla	sillas	chair	chairs
vaso	vasos	glass	glasses
cuchillo	cuchillos	knife	knives
cucharilla	cucharillas	teaspoon	teaspoons
desayuno	desayunos	breakfast	breakfasts
almuerzo	almuerzos	lunch	lunches
cena	cenas	cena	prices
plato	platos	plato	dishes
cortina	cortinas	cortina	curtains
piso	pisos	floor	floors
techo	techos	ceiling	roofs
escuela	escuela	school	school
libro	libros	book	books
cuaderno	cuadernos	notebook	notebooks
lapicero	lapiceros	pencil	pencils

Note some plurals formed with "es":

singular	plural	singular	plural
televisor	televisores	TV	televisions
habitación	habitaciones	bedroom	bedrooms

tren	trenes	train	trains
avión	aviones	plane	planes
mar	mares	mar	mares
pez	peces	fish	fish
luz	luces	light	lights
lápiz	lápices	pencil	pencils
mantel	manteles	mantel	tablecloths
pared	paredes	pared	walls
tenedor	tenedores	fork	forks
habitación	habitaciones	room	bedrooms
papel	papeles	paper	papers
marcador	marcadores	highlighter	markers
jardín	jardines	garden	gardens
flor	flores	flower	flores

*Nouns whose singular forms end in "z", change to "ces" in plural forms.

raíz	raíces	root	roots
lápiz	lápices	pencil	pencils
altavoz	altavoces	loudspeaker	loudspeakers

4.3 Gender of the noun in Spanish

There are two genders in this language to indicate or mention nouns. These are masculine and feminine.

The ending of a noun does not determine its gender. In some cases, these end in the letter "a", but the accompanying definite article may be "el". In the list of articles above, nouns of different genders are mentioned, accompanied by the articles that correspond to them.

Observe a sentence in which different grammatical elements are included.

Example:

sujeto	verbo (conjugado)	complemento	subject	verb (conjugated)	complement
Ana	come	en el restaurante	Ana	eats	in the restaurant

It is also necessary to understand that any complement of a sentence must always be coherent with the verb. Above it is observed that the complement "in the restaurant" is consistent with the verb "eat".

Observe the importance of how to form sentence structures in Spanish:

4.4 Affirmative sentences (indicative mode)

sujeto	verbo	complemento	subject	verb	complement
Carolina	camina	en la ciudad	Carolina	walks	in the city
Los estudiantes	cantan	en el concierto	The students	sing	in the concert
Mis abuelos	cocinan	comida típica	My grandparents	cook	typical food

4.5 Negative sentences (indicative mode)

To form the negative structure of a sentence, you only need to write the word "not" before the verb.

sujeto	palabra de negación "no"	verbo	complemento	subject	negation	verb	complement
Carolina	no	camina	en la ciudad	Carolina	does not	walk	in the city
Los estudiantes	no	cantan	en el concierto	The students	do not	sing	in the concert
Mis abuelos	no	cocinan	comida típica	My grandparents	do not	cook	typical food

4.6 Demonstratives

They are words that point to objects, people, places, situations or animals. The following chart is in Spanish and English.

singular	masculino / femenino	plural	cerca	lejos	male/ female	plural	near	far
este	masculino		x		masculine		x	
esta	femenino		x		female		x	
	masculino	estos (puede ser un grupo de sustantivos masculinos y femeninos)	x		masculine	these (can be a group of masculine and feminine nouns)	x	
	femenino	estas	x		female	is	x	
ese	masculino			x	masculine			x
esa	femenino			x	female			x
eso	neutro		x	x	neutral		x	x
		esos		x		those		x
aquel	masculino			x	masculine			x
aquella	femenino			x	female			x
aquello	neutro		x	x	neutral		x	x
	femenino	aquellas		x	female	those		x
	masculino	aquellos		x	masculine	those		x

As can be seen, the demonstrative "aquello" is neutral, and in most cases it is used with intangible subjects such as ideas and facts.

Aquello que dijiste, ella siempre lo recuerda.	What you said, she always remembers.

4.7 Pronouns

There are many types of pronouns in Spanish, as in all languages. For now, let's study the personal (or subject) type, focused on the subject of the sentence.

Yo	I
Tú	You
Él	He
Ella	She
Usted	You
Nosotros	Us
Nosotras	We

Ustedes	You
Ellos	They
Ellas	They

The function of every (subject) pronoun is to replace a noun; in this case, of subjects.

For example:

Carlos	Él
Beatriz and her family	Ellos
Ana and her friend	Ellas
Carolina and I ("I" is a male)	Nosotros
Carolina and I (I is a female)	Nosotras
Manuel and you	Ustedes

These pronouns are small words whose function is to replace names of people, animals, objects and/ or situations, both singular and plural.

In English there is the pronoun "it" to refer to a situation called "impersonal" in Spanish, since no person performs the action. This does not exist in Spanish; The action is simply expressed automatically starting with the verb in the time that the person chooses to express.

When an idea is expressed in Spanish, it normally begins with the name of the person or subject who carries it out. This is because the pronouns replace them once the idea continues, or the same person continues to be talked about.

Some expressions with personal pronouns are:

Yo trabajo	I work
Tú estudias	You study
Él come	He eats
Ella disfruta	She enjoys
Usted enseña	You teach
Nosotros caminamos	We walk
Nosotras estudiamos	We study
Ustedes comen	You eat
Ellos corren	They run
Ellas cocinan	They cook

As will be seen in this book, the structure of the sentence will follow in all cases. This is a constant for affirmative, negative and question sentences.

There are other types of pronouns in Spanish that help complement different ideas.

4.8 Impersonal sentences in Spanish

In most cases, these types of sentences are as seen below (related to the weather):

Llueve	it rains
Hace frío	it is cold
Está cálido	it is warm
Hace sol	it is sunny
Hace mucha brisa	it is very windy
Está oscuro	it is dark
Está nublado	it is foggy

Practice.

Complete the following sentences and questions with the appropiate definite and indefinite articles:

Esta es _____ nueva casa de Antonio.	This is Antonio's new house
¿Vamos todos a _____ ciudades que ellos promocionan?	Are we all going to the cities they promote?
Benjamín es _____ jefe de Rodrigo	Benjamin is Rodrigo's boss
Ellos son _____ vecinos	They are the neighboors

Practice.

¿Un, uno, una, unos? Look at the phrases and fill in the boxes with the best answer.

Un / una/ unos / unas		
	Ensaladas deliciosas	Delicious salads
	Zapatos confortables	Comfortable shoes
	Buen libro	Good book
	Universidad muy grande	Big University

Underline the correct subject pronoun based on the subjects.

Juan	(Él, ella, usted, nosotros, nosotras, ellos, ellas)
Gabriel y Luis (Gabriel and Luis)	(Él, ella, usted, nosotros, nosotras, ellos, ellas)
Ana y Laura (Ana and Laura)	(Él, ella, usted, nosotros, nosotras, ellos, ellas)
Carolina y yo (Carolina and I)	(Él, ella, usted, nosotros, nosotras, ellos, ellas)
Gustavo y yo (Gustavo and I)	(Él, ella, usted, nosotros, nosotras, ellos, ellas)
Tú y los estudiantes (You and the students)	(Él, ella, usted, nosotros, nosotras, ellos, ellas)

Complete the sentences with the appropiate word according to the gender.

Me gusta vivir en esta_____ Auto/centro comercial/casa	I like living in this_____ Car/mall/house
¡Cuidado con la _____! Lámpara/auto/ abrigo	Be careful with the _____!

Mark with an "x" the correct demonstrative

Los zapatos que quiero son Estos_____ Esta_____	The shoes I want are These_____ This_____

Choose the right option in the following sentences

_____soy la profesora Yo Tú	_____am the teacher I You
_____es tu papa Él Ustedes	_____is your father He You

Chapter 5

5.1 Use of verbs in Spanish

In Spanish, the verbs must be located as expressed by the structure of the sentence in its different forms; a very special one of them is at the beginning of the questions. This does not happen in all cases, but it is important to emphasize that in this case, these verbs must be conjugated at once. To do this, it is very necessary to study each verb and the way in which it is conjugated, according to each tense and subject, whether expressed as a noun or as a pronoun.

5.2 Verbs

In Spanish there are two types of verbs. The regular and the irregular.

5.3 Regular verbs

They are those whose ending is "ar", "er", "ir" in its infinitive form.

5.4 Regular verbs ending in "ar"

These verbs are made up of a root and an ending. Depending on the subject, this ending will change.

Conjugation of verbs ending in "ar"

caminar	(ending form of the verb)	walk
yo camin	o	I walk
tú camin	as	you walk
él camin	a	the road
ella camin	a	she walks
usted camin	a	you walk
nosotros camin	amos	we walk
nosotras camin	amos	we walk
ustedes camin	an	you walk
ellos camin	an	they walk
ellas camin	an	they walk

The other verbs, when conjugated, their endings will change according to the previous table.

Observe some other verbs whose ending/infinitive form is "ar"

saltar	jump
comprar	purchase
ayudar	help
cocinar	cook

5.5 Regular verbs ending in "er"

Some verbs whose ending/infinitive form is "er"

*Conjugation forms of some regular verbs ending in "er" in present.

comer	To eat

Yo como	I eat
Tú comes	You eat
Él come	He eats
Ella come	She eats
Usted come	You eat
Nosotros comemos	We eat
Nosotras comemos	We eat
Ustedes comen	You eat
Ellos comen	They eat
Ellas comen	They eat

Observe some other verbs ending in "er"

comer	eat
correr	run
aprender	learn
responder	answer
vender	sell

5.6 Regular verbs ending in "ir"

The ending forms when conjugated are the same as "er" regular verbs.

Observe some verbs ending in "ir"

compartir	share
asistir	attend
escribir	write
permitir	allow
abrir	open

Tip: Here are some complements that match the above verbs.

Complementos de lugar	Complements of places	Here the preposition "en" is very usual. It is "on, in, at, in English"
En el parque	In the park / at the park	
En la oficina	In the office / at the office	
En la universidad	At the university	
En la biblioteca	At the library	
En el cine	At the movies	
En el supermercado	At the supermarket	
En el jardín	In the garden	
En la escuela	At school	

Practice.

Match the following ideas to make sense

cocinar	en la escuela
compartir	en el parque
aprender	en la cocina

Choose the correct option

Luis_____ frutas en el supermercado Compra Cocina	Luis_____fruits at the supermarket Buys cooks
Eduardo _____la lección Aprende Cocina	Eduardo _____the lesson Learns Cooks

Choose the correct option to make sense

Carolina aprende la lección de idiomas	Carolina learns the language lesson
En la playa_____	At the beach____
En la escuela____	At school_____
En el museo_____	At the museum____
Andrés vende	Andrés sells
Zapatos_____	Shoes____
Biblioteca_____	Library_____
Museo_____	Museum_____

Complete with the correct ending form of the verb

Yo aprend_____	I learn
o, es,emos, en	
Ellos aprend_____	They learn
o, es, emos, en	

Fill in the space with the correct option

Elisa asist_____ a la conferencia	Elisa attends the meeting
o, es,e,imos,en	
Pablo y Juan asist_____ a la conferencia	Pablo and Juan attend the conference
o,es,e,imos,en	

Mark with an "x" the correct option

Pablo	Pablo
Comparte_____	shares
Compartir_____	
Compartes_____	
Manuel y Samuel	
Comparte_____	Manuel and Samuel
Comparten_____	share
Comparto_____	

Chapter 6

6.1 Days of the week and months of the year in Spanish

Complementos de tiempo y frecuencia	Complements of time and frequency	
		When talking about days (same day in plural), the corresponding expression for frequency is: los + day
Los domingos	On Sundays	
Los lunes	On Mondays	
Los martes	On Tuesdays	
Los miércoles	On Wednesdays	
Los jueves	On Thursdays	
Los viernes	On Fridays	
Los sábados	On Saturdays	
		Another form to express frequency forms related with days is through the expression "cada", which is in English "every"
Cada domingo	Every Sunday	
Cada lunes	Every Monday	
Cada martes	Every Tuesday	
Cada miércoles	Every Wednesday	
Cada jueves	Every Thursday	
Cada viernes	Every Friday	
Cada sábado	Every Saturday	
		Or; "todos los+Mondays, etc".
		If the frequency is related with weeks, the expression is "todas las semanas" (every week)
Todos los meses	Every month	If the frequency is related with months, the expression would be "todos los meses" (every month)
Todos los años	Every year	Moreover, if it is related with years, the expression is "todos los años" (every year)

6.2 Irregular verbs

hacer	do
tener	have
conocer	know
mantener	keep
jugar	play
salir	go out

Note the conjugation of these verbs. Its root or any part of them varies.

6.3 Verb "hacer" in present

Yo hago	I do
Tú haces	You do
Él hace	He does
Ella hace	She does
Usted hace	You do
Nosotros hacemos	We do
Nosotras hacemos	We do
Ustedes hacen	You do
Ellos hacen	They do
Ellas hacen	They do

This verb can be used with different activities such as; do homework, make food, do good deeds and even agree on activities with other people.

Examples:

Elizabeth hace el almuerzo todos los días (esto también quiere decir que "prepara" el almuerzo todos los días.	Elizabeth makes lunch every day (this also means she "makes" lunch every day.
Juan siempre hace la limpieza en su casa.	Juan always cleans his house.

6.4 Verb: salir

This verb (also irregular) means "to leave"

Conjugation of regular verbs ending in "er".

It is commonly used along with a the preposition from + place (de+lugar)

Yo salgo de+ lugar	I leave (place)
Tú sales de+lugar	You leave (place)
Él sale de + lugar	He leaves (place)
Ella sale de + lugar	She leaves (place)
Usted sale de + lugar	You leave (place)
Nosotros salimos de + lugar	We leave (place)
Nosotras salimos de + lugar	We leave (place)
Ustedes salen de + lugar	You leave (place)
Ellos salen de + lugar	They leave (place)
Ellas salen de + lugar	They leave (place)

Some regular verbs ending in "ir"

6.5 Verb "subir"

subir	To go up

Note the conjugation of this verb:

Yo subo	I go up
Tú subes	You know
Él sube	He goes up
Ella sube	She goes up
Usted sube	you go up
Nosotros subimos	We went up
Nosotras subimos	we go up
Ustedes suben	you go up

Ellos suben	They go up
Ellas suben	They go up

With this type of verb you can have a complement that refers to an object, along a road, to a car or other means of transportation, at a certain time, among others.

Example:

Elías sube por las escaleras cuando quiere ir a su oficina.	Elías goes up the stairs when he wants to go to his office.

6.6 Verb "ser" /Verb "to be"

Observe again the verb "ser" (to be) has a sense of permanent conditions, altough sometimes it is used for temporary ones.:

*Family and friendship ties (permanent conditions).

Yo soy tu amigo	I am your friend
Tú eres el padre de Ana	You are Ana's father
Él es nuestro jefe	He is our boss
Ella es mi tía	She is my aunt
Usted es su compañero de clases	You are his classmate
Nosotros somos amigos	We are friends
Nosotras somos primas	We are cousins
Ustedes son…	You are…
Ellos son…	They are…
Ellas son…	They are…

Example:

Verónica es la mamá de Gustavo	Verónica is Gustavo's mother

Practice

Complete the spaces with the correct form of the verb "ser"

Benjamín _____mi tío Soy Eres Es	Benjamin _____is my uncle
Carlos y Frank_____ primos Somos Son Es	Carlos and Frank _____cousins
Pedro y yo _____hermanos Es Eres Somos	Peter and I _____brothers

Choose the correct answer

Elías_____un carro Tengo Tenemos tiene	Elías has a car
Martha y Pablo_____muchos amigos. Tenemos Tengo Tienen	Martha and Pblo have many friends

Mark with an "x" the best option

Voy a casa todos_____martes Los___ Las____	I go home every tuesday
Puede visitar a Laura_____lunes Los___ Las_____	You can visit Laura on Mondays

Choose the correct answer

Luisa comparte con sus amigas _____ mañana Cada Siempre Los	Luis shares with her friends_____ morning

| Manuel compra frutas cada_____ <br> martes <br> todos <br> los | Manuel buys fruits every_____
 Tuesday <br> every <br> on |

Fill in with the correct answer

| Yo_____ la ensalada
 Hace
 Hago <br> hacemos | I _____the salad |
| Ellos_____la tarea
 Hacemos
 Hago <br> hacen | They _____the homework |

Choose the correct form

| ¿Benjamín_____los lunes?
 Jugamos
 Juegan <br> juega | Does Benjamin play on Mondays? |
| Elisa y Juan_____ en la calle
 Juegan
 Juego <br> jugamos | Elisa and Juan play on the street |

Chapter 7

7.1 Nationalities, demonyms and provenances

In these cases, nationality or the specific place of origin (demonym) can be exchanged, regardless of whether it is a country, region or place.

Yo soy (nacionalidad/gentilicio)	I am (nationality/demonym)
Tú eres (nacionalidad/gentilicio)	You are (nationality/demonym)
Él es de (lugar)	He is from (place)
Ella es de (lugar)	She is from (place)
Usted es de (lugar)	You are from (place)
Nosotros somos de (lugar)	We are from (place)
Nosotras somos de (lugar)	We are from (place)
Ustedes son (lugar)	You are (place)
Ellos son de (lugar)	They are from (place)
Ellas son de (lugar)	They are from (place)

As seen, the preposition "de" can be used to show the origin of the person or subject.

Observe some countries and their demonyms.

Albania	albanés
Alemania	alemán
Argelia	argelino - na
Argentina	argentino - na
Australia	australiano - na
Bélgica	belga
Bolivia	boliviano - na
Brasil	brasileño - ña brasilero - ra
Bulgaria	búlgaro - ra
Canadá	canadiense
Chile	chileno - na
Colombia	colombiano - na
Costa Rica	costarricense
Croacia	croata
Dinamarca	danés - sa

Ecuador	ecuatoriano - na
Egipto	egipcio - cia
El Salvador	salvadoreño - ña
Eslovaquia	eslovaco - ca
Filipinas	filipino - na
Finlandia	finlandés - sa
Grecia	griego - ga
Guatemala	guatemalteco - ca
Honduras	hondureño - ña
Irlanda	irlandés - sa
Islandia	islandés - sa
Italia	italiano - na
Jamaica	jamaiquino - na
Japón	japonés - sa
Lituania	lituano - na
Luxemburgo	luxemburgués - sa
Malasia	malasio - sa
México	mexicano - na
Nigeria	nigeriano - na
Noruega	noruego - ga
Panamá	panameño - ña
Paraguay	paraguayo - ya
Perú	peruano - na
Portugal	portugués - sa
República Dominicana	dominicano - na
Rusia	ruso - sa
Somalia	somalí
Suecia	sueco - ca
Suiza	suizo - za
Tailandia	tailandés - sa
Uganda	ugandés - sa
Venezuela	venezolano - na
Zambia	zambiano - na

7.2 Professions, occupations

Information can also be exchanged depending on whether the person is a professional or exercises a trade.

Vocabulary of professions and occupations:

abogado	lawyer
arquitecto	architect
actor	actor
actriz	actress
bombero	bomber
cantante	singer
chef	chef
dentista	dentist
enfermera	nurse
escritor	writer
doctor	doctor
fotógrafo	photographer
jardinero	gardener
granjero	farmer
músico	musician
piloto	pilot
profesor	teacher
pintor	painter

Observe examples of sentences with the verb "ser" + the profession or occupation.

Yo soy + profesión / oficio	I am + profession / occupation
Tú eres + profesión / oficio	You are + profession / occupation
Él es + profesión / oficio	He is + profession /occupation
Ella es + profesión / oficio	She is + profession / occupation
Usted es + profesión / oficio	You are + profession /occupation
Nosotros somos + profesión / oficio	We are + profession / occupation
Nosotras somos + profesión / oficio	We are + profession / occupation

Ustedes son + profesión / oficio	You are + profession / occupation
Ellos son + profesión / oficio	They are + profession / occupation
Ellas son + profesión / oficio	They are + profession / occupation

7.3 Indefinites

Algo—--something
Algún —-some
Alguno/alguna-------any
Algunos—some
Algo de—some

Nadie—-nobody
Alguien-somebody

Mucho—---- a lot
Mucha—---- a lot (feminine)
Muchos—-many (masculine, masculine/feminine)
Muchas—-many (feminine)
Poco—-bit (non countable nouns / masculine)
Poca—little (non countable nouns / feminine)
Pocos—few (countable nouns (masculine, masculine/feminine)
Pocas—few (countable nouns/ feminine)

In this section it is necessary to explain the use of these indefinites.

"Mucho" (a lot) is used with non-count nouns to express a large amount of something that, as explained, cannot be counted.

Some examples of non-count nouns are:

time	much time
water	much water
rice	a lot of rice
pasta	a lot of pasta
salad	a lot of salad
food	lots of food

As noted above, time is an "intangible" type noun, but it is also used in this type of expressions.

There are also terms that refer to conditions of a space. For example, "lightness" and "darkness." The expression "have" is used in these cases and in the previous ones.

Hay mucha claridad	There is a lot of clarity
Hay poca oscuridad	There is little darkness

There are also very generalized nouns such as "lighting".

La calle tiene mucho alumbrado	The street has a lot of lighting

With moods and temporal aspects of people, joined to the verb "have", such as:

El bebé tiene mucho sueño	The baby is very sleepy
Ellos tienen poca hambre	They are little hungry
Carlos tiene mucho ánimo	Carlos has a lot of spirit
Ella tiene mucho entusiasmo	She has a lot of enthusiasm

Indefinites are also used with count-type nouns, and these cover many.

El restaurante tiene muchas sillas	The restaurant has many chairs
La casa tiene pocas lámparas	The house has few lamps
Luisa tiene muchos cuadernos	Luisa has many notebooks
Carolina tiene muchos libros	Carolina has many books
Mari tiene muchos amigos	Mari has many friends
Eduardo y Carla tienen muchos tíos	Eduardo and Carla have many uncles

Furthermore, in Spanish, expressions such as probable facts or existence and nonexistence of facts can be used. These are expressed as follows:

No hay mucho qué contar	There is not much to tell
Tengo muchas cosas qué hacer	I have many things to do
Hay mucho qué estudiar	There is a lot to study
Ella tiene mucho qué limpiar	She has a lot to clean
No hay mucho qué ensuciar	There's not much to get dirty

As existence of non-tangible elements:

Aquí hay mucho ruido	There is a lot of noise here
Ellos entablan muchas conversaciones interesantes	They engage in many interesting conversations.
Carlos siempre desea muchas cosas buenas para su familia	Carlos always wishes many good things for his family
En ese país hace mucho frío	It's very cold in that country.
En las playas de esa zona hace mucho calor	It is very hot on the beaches in that area.

7.4 Expression "hay que" (must/obligation)

This expression (also called verbal periphrasis) is used to indicate an obligation to do something without indicating a subject who does it.

Hay que hacer la comida	You have to make the food
Hay que entender bien la lección	You have to understand the lesson well
Hay que buscar los libros	You have to look for the books
Hay que felicitar a los estudiantes	The students must be congratulated

On many occasions, these types of expressions have an expression of time.

Hoy hay que limpiar la casa	Today we have to clean the house
Siempre hay que estudiar la lección	You always have to study the lesson
Nunca hay que olvidar a la familia	We must never forget the family

7.5 Interrogative determiners

These are words used to ask for quantity. In this case, notice how many? (for groups of masculine elements, or masculine and feminine), how many? (for groups of feminine elements); and when they have the letter "s" at the end, the elements are of an accounting type.

Observe the following list of countable nouns (these can be of any type; objects, animals, people, even intangible elements, such as "hours", "days", "months", etc.) In cases like these, sentences are always made in plural:

alfombra	rug
abeja	bee
casa	house

carpeta	file
carta	paper
canción	song
día	day
diente	served
elefante	elephant
elevador	elevator
fuente	fountain
flores	flores
gatos	cats
guantes	gloves
horas	hours
hijos	children
imágenes	images
jarras	jugs
jardínes	gardens
kilos	kilos
limones	lemons
mesas	tables
manzanas	apples
osos	bears
perros	dogs
peces	pieces
regalos	gifts
sandías	watermelons
tortas	a cake
vasos	vases

Determinante interrogativo	sustantivo contable	género	oración	Interrogative determiner	countable noun	gender	sentence
¿Cuántas?	mesas	femenino	¿Cuántas mesas hay en el restaurante?	How many?	tables	female	How many tables are there in the restaurant?

¿Cuántos?	libros	masculino	¿Cuántos platos hay en la mesa?	How many?	books	masculine	How many dishes are on the table?

In the case of non-countable nouns, the interrogative determiners are:

¿Cuánto?	How much?
¿Cuánta?	How much?

Look at the following list of some non-count nouns.

agua	water
tiempo	time
arroz	rice
ensalada	salad

Observe examples:

Determinante interrogativo	sustantivo no contable	género	oración	Interrogative determiner	uncountable noun	gender	sentence
¿Cuánto?	tiempo	masculino	¿Cuánto tiempo ienes para terminar de leer la lección?	How much?	time	masculine	How much time do you have to finish reading the lesson?
¿Cuánta?	agua	femenino	¿Cuánta agua tomas diariamente?	How much?	water	female	How much water do you drink daily?

7.6 Characteristics of one or more people

In Spanish, people are described using words called "adjectives." Adjectives in plural; have "s" at the end. Also, adjectives in Spanish have a masculine or feminine gender. For example, They are tall. Those adjectives that end in the vowel "e" remain the same when used with masculine or feminine subjects. For example, "smart."

Yo soy + inteligente	I am + intelligent
Tú eres + inteligente	You are smarter
Él es + alto	He is + tall
Ella es + baja	She is + short
Usted es + rápido	You are + fast
Nosotros somos + alegres	We are + happy
Nosotras somos + rápidas	We are + fast
Ustedes son + bondadosos	You are + kind
Ellos son + atentos	They are more attentive
Ellas son + atentas	They are more attentive

Other adjectives used for the masculine and feminine gender, ending in "e" are:

eficiente	efficient
ausente	absent
paciente	patient
creyente	believer
elocuente	eloquent

All adjectives are not just used to describe people; also to describe situations, animals and objects. Ordinal numbers and colors can also be used as adjectives. That is, these numbers describe any noun as a position.

7.7 Possessive adjectives

Possessive adjectives replace objects and situations as possession. Look again at the personal pronouns and which possessive adjective corresponds to them, followed by a singular or plural noun:

Yo	mi / mis (plural) + sustantivo	They	my / my (plural) + noun
Tu	tu / tus (plural) + sustantivo	That	your / yours (plural) + noun
Él	su / sus (plural)+ sustantivo	He	his/their (plural)+ noun
Ella	su / sus (plural) + sustantivo	She	his/their (plural) + noun
Usted	su / sus (plural)+ sustantivo	You	his/their (plural)+ noun
Nosotros	nuestro, nuestra, nuestros, nuestras + sustantivo	We	our, our, our, our + noun

Nosotras	nuestro, nuestra, nuestros, nuestras + sustantivo	We	our, our, our, our + noun
Ustedes	su / sus (plural)+ sustantivo	You	his/their (plural)+ noun
Ellos	su / sus (plural) + sustantivo	They	his/their (plural) + noun
Ellas	su / sus (plural) + sustantivo	They	his/their (plural) + noun

Example:

Carolina tiene sus zapatos aquí	Carolina has her shoes here
Los niños quieren conocer a toda su familia	Children want to meet their entire family
Manuel mira a sus aigos desde la ventana	Manuel looks at his friends from the window
Benjamín visita frecuentemente a sus amigos	Benjamin frequently visits his friends
Carlos y Ana estudian en nuestra casa	Carlos and Ana study at our house
Ellos disfrutan hacer sus actividades	They enjoy doing their activities
Luisa tiene mi espejo	Luisa has my mirror

For negative sentences, only the word "not" is added before the main verb.

Carlos y Ana no estudian en nuestra casa	Carlos and Ana do not study at our house

To ask questions, just add question marks at the beginning and end.

¿Benjamín visita frecuentemente a sus amigos?	Does Benjamin frequently visit his friends?

7.8 Possessive pronouns

They are pronouns that replace nouns or not as a form of possession.

Observe the different ways of using them. To do this, it is convenient to make a comparison with possessive adjectives and personal pronouns.

pronombre personal	adjetivo posesivo	pronombre posesivo	ejemplo de pronombre posesivo	personal pronoun	possessive adjective	possessive pronoun	possessive pronoun example
Yo	mi / mis+sustantivo	mío, mía, míos, mías. El mío, la mía, los míos, las mías	Ese auto es mío, esa casa es la mía	They	my/ my+noun	mine, mine, mine, mine. Mine, mine, mine, mine	That car is mine, that house is mine

Tú	tu / tus + sustantivo	tuyo, tuya, tuyos, tuyas, los tuyos, las tuyas	Quiero un libro como el tuyo. Me gustan las casas como la tuya	You	your / your + noun	yours, yours, yours, yours, yours, yours	I want a book like yours. I like houses like yours
Él	su / sus + sustantivo	suyo, suya, suyos, suyas, el suyo, la suya, los suyos, las suyas	Siempre hacemos pinturas como las suyas	He	his/their + noun	yours, yours, yours, yours, yours, yours, yours, yours	We always make paintings like yours
Ella	su / sus + sustantivos	suyo, suya, suyos, suyas, el suyo, la suya, los suyos, las suyas	No quiero un espacio como el suyo; quiero uno más grande.	She	his/their + nouns	yours, yours, yours, yours, yours, yours, yours, yours	I don't want a space like yours; I want a bigger one.
Usted	su / sus + sustantivo	suyo, suya, suyos, suyas, el suyo, la suya, los suyos, las suyas	Tengo un teléfono como los suyos	You	his/their + noun	yours, yours, yours, yours, yours, yours, yours	I have a phone like yours
Nosotros	nuestro / nuestra , nuestros / nuestras + sustantivo	nuestro / nuestra , nuestros / nuestras, 1 nuestro / los nuestros / la nuestra, las nuestras	A Fernando le gustan los libros como los nuestros	We	our / ours, ours / ours + noun	our / ours, ours / ours, ours / ours / ours, ours	Fernando likes books like ours
Nosotras	nuestro / nuestra , nuestros / nuestras + sustantivo	nuestro / nuestra , nuestros / nuestras, 1 nuestro / los nuestros / la nuestra, las nuestras	Ellos siempre compran computadoras como las nuestras.	We	our / ours, ours / ours + noun	our / ours, ours / ours, ours / ours / ours, ours	They always buy computers like ours.

Ustedes	su / sus + sustantivo	suyo, suya, suyos, suyas, el suyo, la suya, los suyos, las suyas	Yo siempre visito a su familia	You	his/their + noun	yours, yours, yours, yours, yours, yours, yours, yours	I always visit his family
Ellos	su / sus + sustantivo	suyo, suya, suyos, suyas, el suyo, la suya, los suyos, las suyas	¿Cuándo compraste sus regalos?	They	his/their + noun	yours, yours, yours, yours, yours, yours, yours, yours	When did you buy his gifts?
Ellas	su / sus + sustantivo	suyo, suya, suyos, suyas, el suyo, la suya, los suyos, las suyas	Espero que ellas traigan a sus familias	They	his/their + noun	yours, yours, yours, yours, yours, yours, yours, yours	I hope they bring their families

7.9 Reflexives pronouns and verbs

Look at the following list of reflexive pronouns. Its function is to be placed before the reflexive/pronominal verb. It should be noted that this type of verb expresses that the action falls on the same subject or person who expresses it.

In the infinitive form, the reflexive/pronominal verbs end in "se".

peinarse	To comb (oneself)
sentarse	To sit (oneself)
mirarse	To look at (oneself)

personal pronoun	reflexive pronoun	conjugated reflexive verb
Yo	me	siento
Tú	te	sientas
Él	se	sienta
Ella	se	sienta
Usted	se	sienta
Nosotros	nos	sentamos

Nosotras	nos	sentamos
Ustedes	se	sientan
Ellos	se	sientan
Ellas	se	sientan

The verb "sentarse" is irregular.

8.0 Verb "gustar" (to like)

This verb indicates enjoyment of something, be it an activity, a meal, one or more objects, among others.

To use it, it is necessary to prefix unstressed personal pronouns, which express that, in the case of "like," said action falls on the subject of the sentence; It is generated by an activity external to it, by a meal, by a landscape, person, etc.

The use of the following phrases is also possible; each one corresponding to each personal pronoun.

	corresponding forms of expressions (next column)			
Yo		Me gusta	I	I like it
Tú		Te gusta	You	you + like it
Él		Le gusta	He	he + likes it
Ella		Le gusta	She	she likes it
Usted		Le gusta	You	you + like it
Nosotros		Nos gusta	We	we + like it
Nosotras		Nos gusta	We	we + like it
Ustedes		Les gusta	You	you + like it
Ellos		Les gusta	They	they + like it
Ellas		Les gusta	They	they + like it

*There are two forms to express:

Me gusta, or a mí me gusta. The same corresponding expressions can be seen in all subjects.

Examples:

Me gusta (or) a mí me gusta cantar	I like to sing	I like singing
Te gusta (or) a ti te gusta estudiar	you like to study	You like studying
Le gusta (or) a él le gusta la sopa	He likes the soup	He likes soup
Le gusta (or) a ella le gusta el parque	She likes the park	She likes the park
Le gusta (or) a ella le gusta el libro	He likes the book	You like that book
Nos gusta (or) a nosotros nos gusta la comida de otros países	We like food from other countries	We like food from other countries
Nos gusta (or) a nosotros nos gusta ir a la playa	We like going to the beach	We like to go to the beach
Les gusta (or) a ellos les gusta pintar la casa	They like to paint the house	They like to paint the house
Les gusta (or) a ellos les gusta escribir	They like to write	They like to write
Les gusta (or) a ellas les gusta caminar en la ciudad	They like to walk in the city	They like to walk in the city

When the noun that causes this perception is plural, the verb "gustar" is also plural, and is expressed as "gustan". In this case, activities are not expressed, but rather tangible or intangible things.

Me gustan las frutas	I like fruits
Te gustan las casas de colores	You like colorful houses
A él le gustan los libros de ese lugar	He likes the books from that place
A él le gustan los vegetales	He likes vegetables
A ella le gustan los abrigos	She likes coats
A nosotros nos gustan las alfombras de este color	We like rugs of this color
A nosotros nos gustan las ciudades frías	We like cold cities
A ellos les gustan las mesas redondas	They like round tables
A ellas les gustan los espacios abiertos	They like open spaces

To express this type of sentences in the negative, as mentioned above, the word "no" is added before "me, te, les, nos, les" + gustar conjugated. This, in cases of singular and plural expressions.

A ellos no les gusta ese deporte	They don't like that sport

They don't like colorful houses	They don't like colorful houses

In the case of questions, the same rule must be followed as in all other cases; place both question marks before and after the sentence in order to show question mark.

| ¿Te gusta estudiar? | Do you like to study? |

In the previous example On the left column, it is understood that previously it was expressed who is being talked about.

8.1 Verb "estar".

This verb "estar" used to express temporary conditions, specifically to talk about the place where someone or some object is (location). This verb is also used to express temporary moods; for example, happy, sad.

For example:

Yo estoy aquí	I'm here
Tú estas en la ciudad	Are you in the city?
Él está triste	He's sad
Ella está feliz	She is happy
Usted está preocupado / a	You are worried
Nosotros estamos felices	We're happy
Nosotras estamos en el parque	We are in the park
Ustedes están en otro país	You are in another country
Ellos están dentro de la casa	They are inside the house
Ellas están fuera de la casa	They are outside the house

The verb "estar" is a single verb, "to be" in English, but in Spanish it is different; since there are two. This verb can be used in different ways and in all verbal tenses, simple and compound. In this book only the simple tenses will be studied.

Another use of this verb is for periods of duration of an action; and this is with the proposition "for", to indicate said period.

Additionally, this verb is used with expressions such as:

"Agree", and this also with names or personal pronouns.

For example:

Yo estoy de acuerdo con (persona o situación)	I agree with (person or situation)
Tú estás de acuerdo con…	You agree with…
Él está de acuerdo con…	He agrees with…
Ella está de acuerdo con…	She agrees with…
Usted está de acuerdo con…	You agree with…
Nosotros estamos de acuerdo con…	We agree with…
Nosotras estamos de acuerdo con…	We agree with…
Ustedes están de acuerdo con…	You agree with…
Ellos están de acuerdo con…	They agree with…
Ellas están de acuerdo con…	They agree with…

This verb "estar" is also used with adjectives related to space such as:

Desorientado (a)	disoriented
Perdido (a)	misplaced

Practice

Choose the correct word, ¿cuánto?, ¿cuántos?, ¿cuánta?, ¿cuántas?

¿_____tiempo tienes para llegar a tu casa?	_____time do you have to get home?
¿_____flores necesita comprar Ana para el ramo?	_____flowers does Ana need to buy for the buch?
¿_____ libros lees al año?	_____books do you read yearly?
¿_____ agua necesitas tomar para tener buena salud?	_____water do you need to drink to be healthy?

Read the conversation.

Los hermanos Samuel y Juan están con su mamá, Elisa.	Samuel and John are with their mother, Elisa.
Juan: Samuel, yo necesito unos zapatos como los tuyos.	Juan: Samuel, I need some shoes like yours.
Samuel: Esa es una buena idea, Juan.	Samuel: That's a good idea, Juan.
Juan: mamá, quiero unos zapatos así, como estos.	Juan: mom, I want some shoes like these.

Elisa: Sí, hijo. Yo siempre compro lo que ustedes necesitan.	Elisa: Sure!, son. I always buy what you both need
Juan: Gracias, mamá	Juan: Thank you, mother
Samuel: Mis zapatos son muy cómodos	Samuel: My shoes are very comfortable
Juan: Lo sé.	Juan: I know
Elisa: Hijos, ¿qué hora es?	Elisa: Sons, what time is it?
Samuel: Son las tres en punto, mamá	Samuel: It's three o' clock, mother
Elisa: ¡Oh! Aún es temprano. Podemos ir a la zapatería	Elisa: Oh! It is still early. We can go to the shoe store.
Juan: Sí, mamá	Juan: Sure!, mother
Elisa: ¿Quieren comer antes de ir?	Elisa: Would you like to eat before going?
Samuel: Sí, yo quiero comer frutas	Samuel: Yes, I want some fruits
Juan: Yo también	Juan: Me too!

Underline possessive adjectives in the above conversation.

Match the correct option.

A_____ me gusta cantar Mí Ella Usted	I like to sing
A ellos _____gusta el teatro Nos Les Me	They like the theater

Choose the correct form

Juan _____triste Estamos Está Estoy	Juan is sad
Carolina y Manuel _____aquí Estamos Están Está	Carolina and Manuel are here

Choose the correct form of possessive adjectives

Este es _____ teléfono El de ella El de él mi	This is my phone
A Carlos le gusta _____ casa Nuestra Sus La de ella	Carlos likes our house

Chapter 8

Verb tenses in the indicative mood:

8.1 Present

The tense expresses actions that are performed in the present, as habits. When actions are performed using regular or non-regular verbs, the endings of these, when conjugated, are; (o, as, a, a, a, amos,amos, an, an,an).

yo	o
tú	as
él	a
ella	a
usted	a
nosotros	somos
nosotras	somos
ustedes	son
ellos	son
ellas	son

This is for regular verbs ending in "ar". Sometimes, this does not happen when expressing sentences in other tenses, since the conjugation between regular and irregular verbs is usually different. There are also, (as in all verb tenses), expressions of time, which help the speaker or reader to define more specifically the moment in which the action will be carried out. This verb tense can be used with all types of complements; those that are related to other subjects; (when introduced, prepositions are generally used) also with place complements, and others. Observe each example, in order to understand the use of this verb tense in more detail.

In this tense, actions such as habits and routines are expressed, which, in most cases, are accompanied by an expression of time in order to emphasize the frequency. As in other languages, in Spanish regular and irregular verbs are conjugated, in the case of regular verbs remaining the root of the verb and changing their endings.

8.2 Affirmative form

The structure of the affirmative sentences is as expressed before:

Subject (this can be composed of one or more nouns)	conjugated verb	complement.

The complement in the present simple can be composed of the forms of expression mentioned above, but there can also be expressions of time in order to emphasize this verbal tense (present). Among the expressions of time in the present, some are:

siempre	always
a veces	sometimes
frecuentemente	frequently
nunca	never
regularmente	regularly

The expressions described above can also be called "adverbs of frequency."

Examples:

Luisa va al supermercado con frecuencia	Luisa goes to the supermarket frequently
Los estudiantes siempre comen en ese restaurante	Students always eat at that restaurant
Manuel estudia en la biblioteca a veces	Manuel studies in the library sometimes
Carlos comparte sus libros regularmente	Carlos shares his books regularly
Eduardo nunca visita el parque	Eduardo never visits the park

It is necessary to emphasize that the last example has a negative time expression through the frequency adverb "nunca" (never).

The present simple can also be used to mean future (this meaning is given by a time expression in future like (tomorrow, a specific time, etc)).

Manuel va a la escuela a las 8:00	Manuel is going to school at 8:00

As seen, the sentence is written in present simple, but the meaning is future "going to".

8.3 Negative form

To form negative expressions of this tense, the word "no" must be added before the first conjugated verb.

Subject (this can be composed of one or more nouns)	no+ conjugated verb	complement.

| Los estudiantes no llegan temprano. | Students do not arrive early. |
| Daniel no come la sopa. | Daniel does not eat the soup. |

8.4 Qualifier adjectives

They describe any noun. For example:

bonito	beautiful
fuerte	strong
bueno	well

8.5 Adverbs

Their function is to modify the verb of a sentence, another adverb, and, sometimes, an adjective. Adverbs include:

*Adverbs of frequency: Mentioned above, they are:

siempre	always
nunca	never
a veces	sometimes
con frecuencia	frequently
rara vez	seldom
frecuentemente	frequently

*Adverbs of manner: describe the way in which an action is performed:

| bien | well |
| mal | bad |

And also those that end with the suffix "mente" (ly). For example.

rápidamente	quickly
fácilmente	easily
lentamente	slowly

There are other types of adverbs in the Spanish language, as well as small prepositions that give meaning to the complement of a sentence.

8.6 Prepositions

They are small words that accompany verbs (or are very close to them) and give meaning referring to time and place.

Among the most common prepositions are:

*Prepositions of place:

dentro	inside
fuera	out
al lado de	beside

*Prepositions of time:

a: When used for time, the correct form is to say: "a la 1:00", or for plural forms: " a las 2:00", and so on. It is also used (among many uses), before names or places; when an action is addressed to any of them. *"Siempre veo a Carlos" *"Voy a la playa"	At *I always see Carlos *I go to the beach
por	for (period of time)
hasta	until

8.7 Direct complement "lo,los" (masculine, singular and plural)

They are used to reflect an action relies over a male or an object (male gender)

Example:

¿Siempre ayudas a tu hermano?	Do you always help your brother?
Sí, siempre lo ayudo	Yes, I always help him

In the above example, "lo" substitutes "tu hermano" (your brother).

¿Alimentas a tus perros en la mañana?	Do you feed your dogs in the morning?
No, yo los alimento en la tarde	No, I feed them in the afternoon

In the above example, "los" substitutes "tus perros" (your dogs). In English, "them".

8.8 Direct complements "la" and "las"

They are used the same way the above pronuns, but for female forms.

Por favor, guarda la carpeta	Please, keep the folder
Sí, ¡claro!	Yes, sure!

¿Lavas las ollas al terminar de usarlas?	Do you wash the pans as soon as you finish using them?
Sí, yo las lavo	Yes, I wash them

8.9 Pronouns of indirect complement

They are used to refer to people/objects actions rely on.

Yo hablo con Juan y le digo cómo hacer bien el trabajo en la computadora	I talk with Juan and tell him how to do the work well in the computer

In the above example, "le" refers to the action that is not directly done over something, but to a person. It is used for singular.

It can also be used for plural, using the pronoun "les".

Martha les hace el desayuno a sus hijos muy temprano en la mañana	Martha makes their sons breakfast very early in the morning

In the above example, "les" refers to "sus hijos" (their sons).

9.0 Questions in present tense

The ways to ask questions in the present tense are:

*They begin with the conjugated verb.

¿Comes siempre en restaurantes?	Do you always eat in restaurants?
¿Compras muchos libros?	Do you buy a lot of books?
¿Estudias en la biblioteca?	You study at the library?
¿Caminas en el parque?	Do you walk in the park?
¿Conoces a muchos estudiantes?	Do you know many students?

*They begin with an information question like:

¿Cuándo?	When?

Examples:

¿Cuándo visitas otros lugares?	When do you visit other places?

¿Cuándo comes en restaurantes?	When do you eat in restaurants?
¿Cuándo juegas con tus amigos?	When do you play with your friends?
¿Cuándo estudias las diferentes materias de la Universidad?	When do you study the different subjects at the University?
¿Cuándo viajas a distintos lugares?	When do you travel to different places?

Examples with "¿Cómo?"

¿Cómo?	How?

¿Cómo estás?	How are you?

Also, this expression is used with another verb related with actions.

¿Cuándo ves las clases de Matemáticas?	When do you see Mathematics classes?
¿Cuándo limpias la casa con tu familia?	When do you clean the house with your family?
¿Cuándo trabajas fuera de la ciudad?	When do you work out of town?
¿Cuándo comes sopa?	When do you eat soup?

Observe questions with where?

¿Dónde?	Where?

¿Dónde estudia Eduardo?	Where does Eduardo study?

¿Dónde come tu familia?	Where your family eats?
¿Dónde lees tus libros favoritos?	Where do you read your favorite books?
¿Dónde paseas los fines de semana?	Where do you walk on weekends?

Observe the questions with "¿por qué?"

¿Por qué?	Why?

¿Por qué lees muchos libros?	Why do you read a lot of books?

¿Por qué ustedes no comen juntos?	Why don't you guys eat together?
¿Por qué Carlos estudia muchos idiomas?	Why does Carlos study many languages?
¿Por qué ellos no limpian la casa?	Why don't they clean the house?
¿Por qué Luis no hace su tarea en la biblioteca?	Why doesn't Luis do his homework in the library?

Observe questions related with time :

¿A qué hora llegas a tu trabajo?	What time do you arrive at work?
¿A qué hora trabajas?	What time do you work?

Observe questions about frequency:

¿Con qué frecuencia?	How often?

¿Con qué frecuencia hablas con tu familia?	How often do you talk to your family?
¿Con qué frecuencia usas tu teléfono?	How often do you use your phone?
¿Con qué frecuencia lees tus libros?	How often do you read your books?
¿Con qué frecuencia viajas?	How often do you travel?
¿Con qué frecuencia van tus amigos de paseo?	How often do your friends go for a walk?

There are other types of questions that follow the same pattern. Observe.

¿Qué?	What?

¿Qué compras en el supermercado?	What do you buy at the supermarket?

¿Quién?	Who?

¿Quién es el profesor?	Who is the teacher?

9.1 The city

There are different types of cities throughout the world. Observe the simple vocabulary of a small city.

restaurante	restaurant
hospital	hospital
farmacia	pharmacy
biblioteca	library
escuela	school
universidad	university
parque	park
cine	movie theater
centro comercial	mall
estadio	stadium
teatro	theater
museo	museum
supermercado	supermarket
plaza	square
edificios	buildings
casas	houses
semáforos	traffic lights
estación de bus	bus station
estación de tren	train station

taxis	taxis

It is important to understand that in this type of exercises (about cities), the verb "quedar" is commonly used.

Observe the meaning of mostly used for referring to cities, as it has many others

quedar	to be located

The usual expression by a tourist or someone new in a city is:

¿Dónde queda +(place)?	Where is + (place) located?

The above expression is used for referring to places (as it is the third person in singular or plural (it/they), it is not (in this sense) common to say quedo, quedas, quedamos, quedan. Those forms are used with the verb "quedarse" (to refer that someone stays somewhere).

Another expression (more formal) is:

Disculpe, por favor, ¿me podría decir dónde queda + (place)?	Excuse me, could you please, tell me where (place) is?

Commonly, other words needed in these types of conversations are those referring to blocks, avenues and streets. Observe:

blocks	cuadras
avenues	avenidas
streets	calles

Observe another type of dialogue:

Turista: Disculpe, ¿dónde queda el hospital más cercano?	Tourist: Excuse me, where is the closest hospital?
Citizen: Queda en la avenida (xxx)	Citizen: It is on (xxx) Avenue
Turista: ¡Muchas gracias!	Tourist: Thanks a lot!

A common expression to refer to the amount of blocks from a certain point of the city is:

Queda a (xx) cuadras	It's (xx) blocks (away) from here

| Queda a (xx) cuadras de aquí | It's (xx) blocks (away) from here |
| Queda a (xx) cuadras de (place) | It's (xx) blocks (away) from (place) |

Practice

Observe the expressions:

El hospital queda a dos cuadras del cine	The hospital is two blocks away from the cinema
La biblioteca queda a 3 cuadras del museo	The library is three blocks away from the museum
El parque queda a 5 cuadras del cine	The park is 5 blocks away from the cinema
La farmacia queda a una cuadra del hospital	The pharmacy is one block away from the hospital
El centro comercial queda a dos cuadras del restaurante	The Mall is two blocks away from the restaurant

When referring to a specific location in terms of Avenues, the expresion is:

| ¿Dónde queda la farmacia? | Where is the pharmacy? |
| En la Avenida (xxx) | It's on (xxx) Avenue |

Practice. Read the dialogue between Rodrigo and a taxi driver.

Rodrigo: Buenas tardes.	Rodrigo: Good afternoon
Taxi driver: Buenas tardes	Taxi driver:Good afternoon
Rodrigo: Voy al teatro más cercano	Rodrigo: I am going to the closest teather
Taxi driver: Sí, ya veo	Taxi driver: Sure! I see
Rodrigo: Aunque quiero saber dónde queda la biblioteca más grande de la ciudad	Rodrigo: Although I would like to know where the biggest library is

Commonly, other words needed in these types of conversations are those referring to blocks, avenues and streets. Observe:

blocks	cuadras
avenues	avenidas
streets	calles

Observe another type of dialogue:

Turista: Disculpe, ¿dónde queda el hospital más cercano?	Tourist: Excuse me, where is the closest hospital?
Citizen: Queda en la avenida (xxx)	Citizen: It is on (xxx) Avenue
Turista: ¡Muchas gracias!	Tourist: Thanks a lot!

Read the questions. Observe different question beginning with question words and some beginning with verbs. Mark with an "x" the ones beginning with question words.

¿Cuándo es tu cumpleaños?	When is your birthday?	
¿Comes siempre a la misma hora?	Do you always eat at the same time?	
¿Por qué no traes tu sweater ahora?	Why don't you bring your sweater now?	
¿Vives cerca o lejos?	Do you live near or far?	
¿A qué hora comen todos ustedes el desayuno?	At what time do you all eat breakfast?	
¿Qué haces los fines de semana?	What do you do on wekends?	

Match the phrases to give meaning to them.

¿Dónde queda	tu cumpleaños?
¿Cuándo es	la ciudad?
¿Te gusta	el cine?

*The above phrases do not have translatons, with the purpose that the reader can accomplish the task.

Mark with an "x" the correct complement

¿_____comes en restaurantes? En el cine Tu casa Siempre
¿Con frecuencia _____ayudas? Corres La Caminas

Chapter 9

9.1 Present + gerund

There is also, within the present tense, the present progressive (not taken into account as a verbal tense), but as expressions that have the main verb ending in "ando", "endo".

This expresses that the actions are carried out at the time they are mentioned. You can ask questions, answers and all kinds of sentences. In the case of adding a time expression, the expression "now" or any synonym for it corresponds.

To do this, it is necessary to use the verb "estar" + any other verb ending in "ando", "endo". If the verb in its infinitive (non-conjugated) form ends in "ar", the continuous form will be "ando". If the verb in infinitive form ends in "er" or "ir", the infinitive form will be "endo".

Example:

cocinar	To cook

Estoy cocinando	I am cooking

comer	To eat

Ella está comiendo	She is eating

subir	to go up

Ellos están subiendo por las escaleras	They are going up the stairs

Look at the following verbs and sentence examples:

Ustedes están ayudando a sus amigos	You are helping your friends
Tú estás manejando el auto	You are driving the car

Now, look at expressions of this type in negative form:

Carlos no está cocinando	Carlos is not cooking
Juan y Luis no están estudiando	Juan and Luis are not studying

Now look at direct questions: These types of questions can begin with the subject that performs the action (noun or pronoun) or with the verb estar.

¿Todos están ayudando a Luis?	Is everyone helping Luis?
¿Manuel y Eduardo están comprando frutas?	Are Manuel and Eduardo buying fruit?

There are verbs that change when used in these types of expressions. Those ending in "er" preceded by a vowel.

traer	trayendo	bring	bringing
caer	cayendo	fall	falling down
leer	leyendo	read	reading
instruir	instruyendo	instruct	instructing
construir	construyendo	build	building
excluir	excluyendo	exclude	excluding
huir	huyendo	run away	running away

There are also, as in all verbal tenses, information questions, but, in this type of expressions, not all information words are coherent. For example, "when?, what time?"

¿Dónde estás comiendo?	Where are you eating?
¿Quién está estudiando con los alumnos?	Who is studying with the students?
¿Por qué estás comprando otro tipo de frutas?	Why are you buying other types of fruits?
¿Con quién estás trabajando?	Who are you working with?
¿Dónde están comiendo?	Where are they eating?
¿Cómo estás cocinando?	How are you cooking?
¿A quién le estás escribiendo?	Who are you writing to?

There is also the option of asking about other subjects like (él, ella, usted, ellos, ellas)

Remember sometimes those subjects may not be included, (due to the conjugation of the verb); sometimes names are, and sometimes the personal pronoun is.

The answers are made according to each question.

*Vocabulary about food

ensalada	salad
lechuga	lettuce
arroz	rice

pasta	pasta
carne	meat
atún	tuna
cereal	cereal
leche	milk
huevos	eggs
queso	cheese
pescado	fish
chicken	pollo
tomate	tomato
cebolla	onion
ajo	garlic
zanahoria	carrot
brocoli	broccoli
papa	potato
limón	lemon
fresa	strawberry
piña	pineapple
sandía	watermelon
banana	banana
cereza	cherry
naranja	orange
uvas	grapes
manzana	apple
piña	pineapple
aguacate	avocado
harina	flour
azúcar	sugar
sal	salt
mantequilla	butter

Verbos usados en la preparación de una receta:	Commonly used verbs when making a recipe:
Mezclar	to mix

poner	to put
licuar	to blend
poner	to put
vertir	to pour
servir	serve

*Vocabulary about restaurant

Before studying the types of conversations about restaurant, it is important to review the proper vocabulary.

mesa	table
cubiertos	silverware
tenedor	fork
cuchara	spoon
cuchillo	knife
taza	cup
plato	dish
mantel	tablecloth
mesero	waiter
mesera	waitress
cocinero	chef
sillas	chairs
servilletas	napkins
vaso	vase
copa	cup
jarra	jug
bebida	drink
comida	food
postre	dessert

carne de res	beef
carne de cerdo	pork meat
pollo	chicken

pescado	fish
comida del mar	sea food
arroz	rice
pasta	pasta
sopa	soup
ensalada	salad
vegetales	vegetables
frutas	fruits
agua	water
jugos de frutas	fruit juices
pan	pan

entradas	appetizer
plato principal	main dish
postres	desserts

Common verbs for restaurant expressions:

cortar	To cut
picar	To cut
comer	To eat
beber	To drink
probar	To taste
servir	To serve

9.2 Preterite (past)

This tense describes actions that already occurred at a certain time in the past. Sentences can also include expressions of time. There are also, like in other tenses, specific ones that help the speaker or reader emphasize or understand the expressions better. Affirmative, negative and differente types of questions can be done, like in all tenses.

Observe the time expressions mostly used for this tense:

ayer	yesterday
Hace dos días/mese/años	Two days/months/years ago
La semana pasada	Last week
El mes pasado	Last month
El año pasado	Last year

9.3 Affirmative sentences in the past

Luis comió ensalada ayer	Luis ate salad yesterday

El profesor dió la clase la semana pasada	The teachers taught the class last week

9.4 Negative sentences in the past

They are structured just by adding the word "no" before the main verb in sentences.

Manuel no visitó a su familia el mes pasado	Manuel did not visit his family last month

Carlos no entendió la lección ayer	Carlos did not understand the lesson yesterday

9.5 Questions in past

¿Luis comió ensalada ayer?	Did Luis eat salad yesterday?

¿Los profesores dieron la clase de español la semana pasada?	Did the teachers teach Spanish class last week?

9.6 Preterite imperfect + gerund / Past + gerund

Notice what the expressions look like continuously in the past (these types of expressions are called preterite imperfect). They have to be formed with the verb "estar" in the preterite imperfect tense, and, in Spanish, this is "estaba" that is past, these forms of verbs conjugated according to the person + any verb in continuous form; that is, ending in "endo", "ando".

9.7 Affirmative sentences

Yo estaba	I was
Tú estabas	You were
Él estaba	He was
Ella estaba	She was
Usted estaba	you were
Nosotros estábamos	We were
Nosotras estábamos	We were
Ustedes estaban	You were
Ellos estaban	They were
Ellas estaban	They were

Examples:

Elizabeth estaba trabajando ayer	Elizabeth was working yesterday
Juan estaba escuchando música con sus hermanos a las 4:30	Juan was listening to music with his brothers at 4:30
Gabriel estaba cocinando con sus familia ayer	Gabriel was cooking with his family yesterday

9.8 Negative sentences

Elizabeth no estaba trabajando ayer	Elizabeth was not working yesterday
Juan no estaba escuchando música con sus hermanos a las 4:30	Juan was not listening to music with his brothers at 4:30
Gabriel no estaba cocinando con sus familia ayer	Gabriel was not cooking with his family yesterday

On many occasions, this type of sentence is completed with another in the past tense, and their union is made with the word "cuando" (when). For example;

| Raquel estaba cocinando cuando su mamá llegó. | Raquel was cooking when her mother arrived. |
| Eduardo estaba leyendo cuando Leonardo la interrumpió. | Eduardo was reading when Leonardo interrupted her. |

Practice

Observe the two columns. Match actions coherently.

¿Dónde están comiendo	con Martha?
¿Quién está estudiando	estudiando ahora?
¿Dónde está	estás cocinando?
¿Por qué estás	Elisa y John?
¿Cómo	trabajando Juan?

Practice. Read the following recipe.

Example:

Limonada:	Lemonade:
Ingredientes:	Ingredients:
*10 limones	*10 lemons
*2 litros de agua	*2 liters of water
*Azúcar al gusto.	*Some sugar
Preparación:	How to prepare it:
*Verter el jugo de los limones en el agua.	*Pour the lemon juice in the water.
*Añadir el azúcar al gusto.	*Add the sugar as wish.
*Mix.	*Mezclar.

Practice.

Read the following sentences about imperfect+gerund. Underline the verbs in this form.

| Elías estaba jugando con sus amigos ayer a las 6:00 de la tarde | Elias was playing with his Friends at 6:00 in the evening |

¿Beatriz estaba cocinando cuando llegaste?	Was Beatriz cooking when you arrived?
¿Por qué los amigos de Juan estaban escuchando la lección en la mañana?	Why were Juan's Friends listening to the lesson in the morning?
¿Manuel y Ana estaban comiendo en casa con sus hijos el día del cumpleaños de Ana?	Were Manuel and Ana eating at home with their kids on Ana's birthday?
¿Cuándo estaban Miguel y su familia limpiando su casa?	When were Miguel and his family cleaning thir house?

Match the sentences to give the correct meaning

¿Por qué	estabas en el restaurante?
¿Cuándo	estabas comiendo en el restaurante ayer?
¿A quién	le gusta añadir ingredientes a la limonada?

Match the phrases with the correct form

¿Los profesores	ayer?
¿Preparaste la ensalada	comieron en la escuela?
¿Fuiste de viaje	la semana pasada?

*The above sentences do not have translations. It is expected the reader understands and matches.

Read the verbs (infinitive form) with their past forms

| cortar | Yo corté, tú cortaste, él cortó, ella cortó, usted cortó, nosotros cortamos, nosotras cortamos, ustedes cortaron, ellos cortaron, ellas cortaron |
| picar | Yo piqué, tú picaste, él picó, ella picó, usted picó, nosotros picamos, nosotras picamos, ustedes picaron, ellos picaron, ellas picaron |

*Both verbs are used to express "to cut".

Write "T" for true and "F" for false.

Time expression	Meaning	"T" or "F"
ayer	yesterday	
La semana pasada	hoy	
El mes pasado	last month	
El año pasado	this year	

Chapter 10

10.1 Future

Observe how verbs end in future tense:

Yo	é
Tú	ás
Él	á
Ella	á
Usted	á
Nosotros	emos
Nosotras	emos
Ustedes	án
Ellos	án
Ellas	án

The above ending formas are for all types of regular verbs; those ending in "ar", "er" and "ir".

Example: verb "caminar"

Yo caminaré	I will walk
Tú caminarás	You will walk
Él caminará	He will walk
Ella caminará	She will walk
Usted caminará	You will walk
Nosotros caminaremos	We will walk
Nosotras caminaremos	We will walk
Ustedes caminarán	You will walk
Ellos caminarán	They will walk
Ellas caminarán	They will walk

When the verb is irregular, in some cases, the endings will remain as the previous ones.

An example of this is the verb "querer" (to want).

Yo querré	I will want
Tú querrás	You will want

Él querrá	He will want
Ella querrá	She will want
Usted querrá	You will want
Nosotros querremos	We will want
Nostras querremos	We will want
Ustedes querrán	You will want
Ellos querrán	They will want
Ellas querrán	They will want

Other irregular verbs:

*Jugar: to play

Observe the conjugation of this verb in the future, although in the present it is different, in the future it retains its root and its corresponding endings.

Yo jugaré	I'll play
Tú jugarás	You will play
Él jugará	He will play
Ella jugará	She will play
Usted jugará	You will play
Nosotros jugaremos	We will play
Nosotras jugaremos	We will play
Ustedes jugarán	You will play
Ellos jugarán	They will play
Ellas jugarán	They will play

*Traer: to bring

Yo traeré	I'll bring
Tú traerás	You will bring
Él traerá	He will bring
Ella traerá	She will bring
Usted traerá	You will bring
Nosotros traeremos	We will bring
Nosotras traeremos	We will bring

Ustedes traerán	You will bring
Ellos traerán	They will bring
Ellas traerán	They will bring

As explained above, the simple future tense expresses actions that will be performed in the future. When actions are performed using regular or non-regular verbs, the endings of these, when conjugated with each subject, are; (ré, rás, rá, rá, rá, emos, emos, rán, rán, rán); (the previous sequence is based on the subject pronouns chart). Sometimes, this does not happen when expressing sentences in other tenses, since the conjugation between regular and irregular verbs is usually different. There are also, (as in all verb tenses), expressions of time, which help the speaker or reader to define more specifically the moment in which the action will be carried out. This verb tense can be used with all types of complements; those that are related to other subjects; (when introduced, prepositions are generally used) also with place complements, and others. Observe each example, in order to understand the use of this verb tense in more detail.

Expressions of the future with complements from other people.

Luisa trabajará con su familia	Luisa will work with her family
Mari y Juan comerán mañana con Ana en el restaurante	Mari and Juan will eat tomorrow with Ana at the restaurant
Mis amigos y yo estudiaremos con nustros profesores	My friends and I will study with our teachers
¿Cuándo visitarás a tu familia con Mari?	When will you visit your family with Mari?
Benjamín limpiará su casa con su familia	Benjamin will clean his house with his family
Leonardo preparará el desayuno con Juan	Leonardo will prepare breakfast with Juan

Expressions of the future with complements of place.

In this type of expressions, the preposition "in" is used, to then use a specific place where the action will be performed.

Todos estudiarán en la nueva biblioteca	Everyone will study in the new library
Ellos comprarán la nueva computadora en la tienda en esa avenida	They will buy the new computer in the store on that avenue
Elizabeth comerá en el restaurante	Elizabeth will eat at this restaurant
¿Disfrutarán tus amigos en el parque	Will your friends enjoy themselves in the park?
¿Con qué frecuencia correrás en ese estadio?	How often will you run in that stadium?
¿Cuántos libros comprarás en esa librería?	How many books will you buy in that bookstore?

Expressions in the future with the preposition "para". This type of expression is used in order to express a purpose of performing the future action. This expression can also be used to define to whom the future action will be performed.

Observe those with a sense of future purpose.

Luis comprará los ingredientes para preparar el pastel	Luis will buy the ingredients to prepare the cake
Los amigos de Laura irán a la estación de tren para comprar los tickets	Laura's friends will go to the train station to buy tickets
Andrés y Ana estudiarán mucho para entender las nuevas lecciones	Andrés and Ana will study hard to understand the new lessons

Observe expressions with the preposition "for" in the sense of defining to whom an action will be performed.

Manuel escribirá muchos poemas para su mamá	Manuel will write many poems for his mother
¿Comprarás juguetes para los niños mañana?	Will you buy toys for the children tomorrow?
¿Cocinarás esta tarde para tu familia?	Will you cook this afternoon for your family?

10.2 Future + gerund

If you want to know the form of expressions such as future progressive; (future + gerund), it can be seen in examples such as the following:

Gustavo estará comiendo a las 12:00 en ese restaurante	Gustavo will be eating at 12:00 noon in that restaurant

It is then observed that the action will be in progress. Sometimes the moment in which it will be carried out is expressed, and on other occasions the complement will be different.

Other examples (even the moment in which the action will be carried out can be written at the beginning)

Luis y su familia estarán visitando muchos museos durante sus vacaciones.	Luis and his family will be visiting many museums during their vacations.
El miércoles, Susana estará tomando fotografía en el jardín con sus amigos.	On Wednesday, Susan will be taking pictures in the garden with her friends

Notice the negative sentences. Like all the previous ones, you should only write the word "no" before the verb estar in the future.

Luis y su familia no estarán visitando muchos museos durante sus vacaciones	Luis and his family won't be visiting many museums during their vacation.
El miércoles, Susan no estará tomando fotos en el jardín con sus amigos	On Wednesday, Susan will not be taking pictures in the garden with her friends

To ask questions you can follow the parameters set out in all the previous verb tenses; begin with the once conjugated verb or the main subject of the question.

10.3 Verbal periphrasis "ir +a"

It is necessary to explain that a verbal periphrasis is a combination of words that make up a short expression. Its purpose is to function as a constant in the verb that is used, which will be conjugated according to the person who is the subject of the sentence.

This expression has a future meaning, and its complement could be different; from a very near or distant future. Also, you can omit the subject of the sentence once the conjugated verb is observed, in which said subject is always implicit, although in the cases of he, she and you it is convenient to identify said subject, since the conjugation is the same.

¿Por qué vas a estudiar ahora?	Why are you going to study now?
¿Por qué vas a comer temprano?	Why are you going to eat early?
¿Dónde va a hablar él mañana?	Where is he going to talk tomorrow?
¿Cuándo ella va a comer a ese restaurante?	When is she is going to eat at that restaurant?

Él va a hablar mañana en la conferencia.	He is going to speak tomorrow at the conference

10.4 Offerings in Spanish

To offer in Spanish, there are different types of expressions. Observe some in simple present form.

¿Quieres?	Would you like?	You (singular)
¿Quieren?	Would you like?	You (plural)

The above expressions can be used followed by a noun :

¿Quieres helado?	Would you like some ice cream?
¿Quieren un libro?	Would you like a book?

There is also the possibility to write the offering expression "querer" plus a verb. In these cases, it is an invitation to do something, to have something to eat, etc.

¿Quieres comer cereal?	Do you want to eat some cereal?
¿Quieren ir de paseo con nosotros?	Do you want to go sightseeing with us?
¿Quieren cocinar en mi casa?	Do you (plural) want to cook in my house?
¿Ellas quieren venir al parque a disfrutar?	Do they want to come to the park enjoying?
¿Ustedes quieren comer con nosotros en el restaurante?	Do you want to eat with us at the restaurant?

Also, according to the situation and intonation, the invitations with the subject (ellas, ellos) can be seen as a question or more like an invitation.

10.5 Conditional expressions

Conditional forms indicates that a verb is described under a condition. In most cases, these verbs end in "ía", but it is convenient to show each ending, according to the subject.

Verb: "Ir" (to go)

Yo iría	I would go
Tú irías	You would go
Él iría	He would go
Ella iría	She would go
Usted iría	You would go
Nosotros iríamos	We would go
Nosotras iríamos	We would go
Ustedes irían	You would go
Ellos irían	They would go
Ellas irían	They would go

Normally, this type of verb form is preceded by another conditional sentence in which the word "if" + subject + verb is used (in certain tenses).

Observe sentences with the verb forms described above in the table, but alone.

Verb: entrenar (to train)

Yo entrenaría a mi mascota	I would train my pet.

Verb: limpiar (to clean)

¿Limpiarías bien la casa?	Would you clean the house well?

Verb: cuidar (to care)

¿Cuidarías bien a las mascotas?	Would you take care of the pets?

Notice the following exception. It is an irregular verb.

salir	To go out

Yo saldría	I would go out
Tú saldrías	You would go out
Él saldría	He would go out
Ella saldría	She would go out
Usted saldría	You would go out
Nosotros saldríamos	We would go out
Nosotras saldríamos	We would go out
Ustedes saldrían	You would go out
Ellos saldrían	They would go out
Ellas saldrían	They would come out

10.6 Give and ask for advice

In this lesson related to giving and asking for advice, we see how these expressions should be used with another verb unconditionally. This is "should". It is necessary to combine it with each person, in the following way:

Yo	debería	I	should
Tú	deberías	You	should

Él	debería	He	ought to
Ella	debería	She	ought to
Usted	debería	You	ought to
Nosotros	deberíamos	We	should
Nosotras	deberíamos	We	should
Ustedes	deberían	You	should
Ellos	deberían	They	should
Ellas	deberían	They	should

These forms of conjugation, or this conjugated verb, are used followed by another verb (any) in base or infinitive form. Sometimes, a need or expression of illness or problem is usually expressed.

Look at the following examples:

a)"Me duele la cabeza"	a) "My head hurts"
b) ¡Deberías ir al doctor!	b) You should go to the doctor!
a) "Ana se siente muy mal. Está muy triste"	a) "Ana feels very bad. "He is very sad"
b) Ell debería llamar a sus amigos	b) He should call his friends
"Los estudiantes no entienden esa materia"	a)"Students don't understand this subject"
b)Ellos deberían estudiar más	b)They should study more
"Gustavo tiene hambre"	a)"Gustavo is hungry"
b)Él debería ir a comer al restaurante.	b)He should go eat at the restaurant.
"Luis no quiere ayudar a su mamá"	"Luis doesn't want to help his mother"
Él debería ayudarla	He should help her
"Carlos se rompió la pierna en su bicicleta"	a)"Carlos broke his leg on his bicycle"
b)Debería ir al doctor	b)I should go to the doctor

These types of sentences can also be done in negative and question forms.

Among other expressions of basic forms of Spanish, it is necessary to emphasize those that have a meaning of skills. These are expressed through the verbs "poder" and "saber".

10.7 Verb poder (to be able to)

This verb expresses that the subject has the ability to carry out an activity or is very excellent at speaking other languages, playing musical instruments, doing crafts, cooking, practicing a sport with excellence, driving a means of transportation, teaching classes, and singing, among others.

The verb "poder" is an irregular verb, and its conjugation in the present, past and future is very different, even this verb is used conditionally, ending in "ía, ías, ía, ía, ía, íamos, ían, ían " (forms according to each subject within the table of personal pronouns).

Observe the conjugation in present:

Yo puedo	I can
Tú puedes	You can
Él puede	He can
Ella puede	She can
Usted puede	You (formal) can
Nosotros podemos	We can
Nosotras podemos	We can
Ustedes pueden	You (plural) can
Ellos pueden	They can
Ellas pueden	They can

After these conjugation forms, it is possible to add a verb infinitive form, a negative sentence or a question. It is important to state that the verb "poder" refers to abilities and permissions.

Yo puedo saltar la cuerda	I can jump the rope
Tú puedes hablar francés	You can speak French
Él puede nadar	He can swim
Ella puede tocar el piano	She can play the piano
Usted puede manejar un auto	You can drive a car
Nosotros podemos ir a la biblioteca	We can go to the library
Nosotras podemos hablar muchos idiomas	We can speak many languages

10.8 Verb saber: to know

The verb "saber" also expresses the ability or capacity to carry out an activity. In most cases, this verb is accompanied by another that emphasizes skill. For example; know how to cook, know how to speak other languages, know how to cook, know how to drive a car, know how to teach, know how to swim, know how to play musical instruments, know how to sew clothes, know how to draw, know how to make crafts, know how to teach others, know how to lead a conference, know how to decorate , knowing how to clean the house, knowing how to talk to others, etc.

Observe the conjugation of "saber" in present simple. It is an irregular verb.

Yo sé	I know
Tú sabes	You know
Él sabe	He knows
Ella sabe	She knows
Usted sabe	You know
Nosotros sabemos	We know
Nosotras sabemos	We know
Ustedes saben	You know
Ellos saben	They know
Ellas saben	They know

Examples:

Ellas saben cocinar muy bien	They know how to cook very well

Eduardo no sabe nadar	Eduardo does not know how to swim

¿Martha sabe cómo usar la aspiradora?	Does Martha know how to use the vacuum cleaner?

Sí, ella sabe usarla	Yes, she knows how to use it
No, ella no sabe usarla	No, she does not know how to use it.

As seen, the answers can be "sí"+ complement, "no" + complement.

There are some other different expressions in Spanish to reply when being asked a question. These are:

quizás	maybe
probablemente	probably
no lo sé	I don't know

10.9 Other forms of expressions

Observe the use of this verb "saber" in past:

Yo supe	I knew
Tú supiste	You knew
Él supo	He knew
Ella supo	She knew
Usted supo	You knew
Nosotros supimos	We knew
Nosotras supimos	We knew
Ustedes supieron	You knew
Ellos supieron	They knew
Ellas supieron	They knew

After them, there is the possibility to write, either a verb in infinitive form, or an expression which means "how to"+ verb in infinitive form.

Los estudiantes (ellos) supieron tocar la guitarra durante el concierto	The students (they) knew how to play the guitar during the concert
Carolina supo que sus amigos llegaron a las 10:00 am	Carolina knew that her friends arrived at 10:00 am
Los amigos de Francisco supieron que él comería con ellos	Francisco's friends knew that he would eat with them

Observe the conjugation form of "saber" in future.

Yo sabré	I will know
Tú sabrás	You will know
Él sabrá	He will know
Ella sabrá	She will know
Usted sabrá	You will know

Nosotros sabremos	We will know
Nosotras sabremos	We will know
Ustedes sabrán	You will know
Ellos sabrán	They will know
Ellas sabrán	They will know

The complements for these conjugations is:

Benjamín sabrá comprar en el suprmercado	Benjamin will know how to buy at the supermarket
Carlos y Luis sabrán cocinar	Carlos and Luis will know how to cook
Ellos sabrán nadar en la playa	They will know how to swim in the beach

The verb "conocer" is also used to express that the subject knows about certain real facts or not.

For example; knowing that something exists, knowing a reality (that everyone knows about), knowing someone's name, knowing the future, knowing the past, knowing the location of a country, city, continent, landscape, commercial places, where someone is, among others.

On the other hand, there is the verb "conocer", and this is used to express that the subject of the sentence knows a person by reference, or has not treated them much; also that the subject has visited some place in the past, or will visit it in the future. This verb is also used to express that the subject knows about realities, has been introduced to a person, has seen or visited some place, country, region, or continent.

Among other verbs of real importance when speaking Spanish, there are:

Those to express opinions:

Pensar: This verb is used to express opinion and give recommendation with the aim that the same subject or others do something. It is also an introduction to depression that focuses on giving some advice. When used in the form of a question, this indicates that the subject is asking for some kind of advice as well. The conjugation is as follows:

Yo pienso	I think
Tú piensas	You think
Él piensa	He thinks
Ella piensa	She thinks
Usted piensa	You think

Nosotros pensamos	We think
Nosotras pensamos	We think
Ustedes piensan	You think
Ellos piensan	They think
Ellas piensan	They think

Normally, the above expressions are followed by expressions like:

Que + sujeto + verbo + complemento	That +subject+ verb + complement
Que + demostrativo + verbo + complemento	That + demonstrative + verb + complement

Observe:

Yo pienso que caminar es bueno	I think that walking is good
Tú piensas que esta comida es deliciosa	You think that this meal is delicious
Él piensa que aquel carro es bonito	He thinks that that car is beautiful

Considerar: This verb has the same use as the verb "pensar" (to think) and is regular; once it is conjugated, it maintains its base form and its endings follow the rule of conjugations. Both verbs "pensar" and "considerar" are generally followed by the connector "que"; This introduces a secondary idea, either as advice or as reality. It is necessary to study the use of these verbs in a very detailed way, since they are of great importance and widely used in Spanish.

Yo considero	I consider
Tú consideras	You consider
Él considera	He considers
Ella considera	She considers
Usted considera	You consider
Nosotros consideramos	We consider
Nosotras consideramos	We consider
Ustedes consideran	You consider
Ellos consideran	They consider
Ellas consideran	They consider

Opinar (to opine): It is another verb that is followed in most cases by the connector "que" (that), and is used to introduce a secondary expression and/or give advice.

*Verb quedarse: means that the subject spends some time in a specific place. It also means that the subject gets off some public transport, makes a stopover during his trip, and although it does not have the same meaning, this verb also expresses a change of mood or reaction after an action seen by the subject (In many cases, a expression of astonishment)

Observe the conjugation of this verb:

yo	me quedo
tú	te quedas
él	se queda
ella	se queda
usted	se queda
nosotros	nos quedamos
nosotras	nos quedamos
ustedes	se quedan
ellos	se quedan
ellas	se quedan

Observe the use of this verb as "to stay" in a place or to leave a transport.

Cuando viajo a otros países, me quedo en las ciudades principales	When I travel to other countries, I stay in the main cities
Manuel fue al centro de la ciudad, y se quedó en la capital	Manuel went downtown the city, and stayed in the capital
Benjamin viajará a la playa en autobús, y se quedará en la parada de allí	Benjamin will travel to the beach by bus, and he will stay at the bus stop

Other expressions:

Con su familia	With his/her family
En (lugar)	At (place)

*Acostumbrarse: This verb expresses that the subject of the sentence acquires a way of doing something, a lifestyle, or some change in their previous habits. It is normally followed by the preposition "a" + verb that indicates the new habit.

*Peinarse: This verb indicates that the subject, in most cases, performs the action on itself.

*Enfocarse: This verb means that the subject acquires greater concentration in relation to some habit or activity, and it is convenient for him, in most cases.

*Sentarse: Involves the action of taking a seat.

All of these verbs are accompanied by little words called "reflexive pronouns" (explained above).

11.0 Expressions to give orders

Expressions to give orders in Spanish generally have a structure that begins directly with the verb (if affirmative) or with the negation word (if negative).

Normally, this type of sentence is made in the present tense, and from a point of view oriented towards the second person of the singular "tú" and the plural "ustedes". It should not be done directly using another approach or subjects.

This type of sentence is also called imperative sentences.

11.1 Predictions and inferences

This type of expressions includes several verb tenses; For example, you can often begin with the present tense and then continue with an expression of consequence in the future.

There are also expressions that reflect the past of something (inferences of the past), but in the present tense.

Examples

Present + future	
Creo que va a llover	I believe it will rain
¿Piensas que va a hacer sol esta tarde?	Do you think it is going to be sunny today?
Me parece que hoy será un día muy divertido	I think it will be a funny day today
Creo que mañana hará sol	I believe tomorrow it will be sunny
Luis piensa que sus hermanos irán al parque esta tarde	Luis thinks his brothers will go to the park this afternoon
Los estudiantes creen que habrá muchas oportunidades de estudio en el futuro	The students believe that there will be many study opportunities in the future

Present + past	
Carlos piensa que su hermano sí fue a la escuela	Carlos thinks his brother did go to school
Mis amigos creen que hizo mucho más frío en el invierno pasado	My friends believe the weather was too much colder last winter

La familia piensa que nuestros invitados sí llegaron a tiempo a la reunión	The family thinks our guests did arrive on time to the meeting
Todos creen que el profesor explicó muy bien la clase	Everyone believes the teacher explained the class very well
Los visitantes piensan que el paseo estuvo muy divertido	The visitors think that the tour was very funny
Luisa piensa que todos obtuvieron excelentes notas	Luisa thinks they all got excellent grades

Practice

From the second column, write "T" for true conditional forms and "F" for false conditional forms.

		"T" or "F"
escribir	escribirá	
comer	comería	
jugar	jugará	
trabajar	trabajaría	

Underline the verbal periphrasis "ir a" conjugated.

Sé que Sandra va a jugar con sus hermanos en el parque	I know Sandra is going to play with her brothers at the park
¿Por qué todos ellos van a cuidar a las mascotas en la tarde?	Why are they all going to care for th pets in the afternoon?
¿Gustavo va a caminar mañana por toda la ciudad?	Is Gustavo going to go walking through the whole city tomorrow?

Match the correct phrases in Spanish

Pablo piensa que	la casa es muy grande
Ellos piensan que	pensamos que tus notas son muy buenas
Nosotros	que ellos son muy felices?
¿Ustedes pensaron	María es su nueva profesora

Write "T" if the sentence is correct, "F" for if it is incorrect.

Carla supo manejar el auto	
Carla preparó manejar el auto	

Mark "x" in the correct sentence

¿Quieres tomar jugo?	
¿Quieres tomé un jugo?	

Complete the sentences with the correct form of the verb

Manuel _____ mañana Trabajó Trabaja Trabajará	Manuel _____tomorrow

Chapter 11

11.1 Preposition "por" (as a consequence)

The preposition "por" means a consequence (affirmative or negative), based on previous experiences.

Examples:

Todos tus amigos fueron al viaje. Por eso, no habrá clases hoy	All your relatives went on a trip. For that reason, there will not be classes today
La familia de Juan comió en el restaurante. Por eso, no fue al supermercado de compras	Juan's family ate at the restaurante. For that reason, they did not go buying to the supermarket
Nancy viajó a visitar muchos países. Por eso, Carolina está trabajando en su lugar.	Nancy traveled to visit many countries. For that reason, Carolina is working instead of her.

11.2 Por (periods of time)

The preposition "por" is used for period of time in expressions based in any tense.

Read the following ideas.

Elisa viajará a otros continentes por 6 meses	Elisa will travel to other continents for 6 months
Los amigos de Lucas comieron los platos típicos de la región por 10 días	Lucas's friends ate the typical plates of the region for 10 days
La abuela de George visitó a sus nietos por 5 horas.	George's grandmother visited her grand sons for 5 hours
Todos los invitados de Sebastián hablaron por 2 días durante el viaje	All Sebastian's guests talked for 2 days during the trip

11.3 Pasive voice

The passive voice is one of the forms of expressions in Spanish. There are two types of voices or ways of expressing themselves: the active one, whose form is:

subject	verb	complement composed of some of the following elements: *preposition. *other subjects/objects

Example:

Los estudiantes	leen	ese libro
The students	read	that book

On the other hand, to form the passive voice, it is always necessary to include the verb "ser". In this book, the active and passive forms of the present, past and future tenses are studied.

Notice how the expression described above looks like in passive voice:

Ese libro	es	leído	por	los estudiantes
That book	is	read	by	the students

It is necessary to explain the formula to understand the passive voice. Furthermore, this type of expression is usually very formal in use and is not sometimes literary.

Before, the object of the sentence, which becomes the subject	verb "to be" (in the same tense of the active form, if it appears before)	verb in participle form (ido,ado)	phrase that indicates who performs the action or who performed or will perform it	the subject of the sentence has become its object in the form of passive voice

In the previous example both active and passive forms were shown in the present tense. Notice how this form is used in the past tense.

Active voice

Los	estudiantes	leyeron	ese	libro
The	students	read	that	book

Passive voice

Ese	libro	fue	leído	por	los estudiantes
That	book	was	read	by	the students

It is also necessary to emphasize that these examples are based on changes of expressions from active to passive, since it is a way of studying them, and that the verbs necessary for these types of sentences are those called transitives. Transitive verbs are those that are accompanied by a subject (person, thing, or something non-tangible) on which the action falls. Typically, there may be directly passive forms in real environments.

Notice the future form of the previous example:

Active voice

Los	estudiantes	leerán	ese	libro
The	students	will read	that	book

Passive voice

Ese libro	será	leído	por	los	estudiantes
That book	will be	read	by	the	students

Is there a passive voice for gerund verb forms?

The answer is yes.

In that sense, the passive forms are the following:

Ese	libro	está	siendo	leído	por	los estudiantes
That	book	is	being	read	by	the students

It is added before the progressive form of "ser", the verb "estar", plus the verb "leer" in the participle. Then, the complement.

Note that it is a form of progressive expression that takes as its subject the object normally expressed in the active voice.

present (active)				
The students	are	reading	that	book

11.4 Ya

This expression indicates the accomplishment of an action. It also indicates that something will occur within a short time.

Cumplimiento de una acción en un pasado reciente	Accomplishment of an action in a recet past	
Enrique ya hizo la comida	Enrique already made the food	
Pablo y Juan ya usaron sus computadoras	Pablo and Juan already used their computers	
Elizabeth ya se graduó de doctora	Elizabeth already graduated a a doctor	
Carlos ya habló con la familia de Ana	Carlos already talked with Ana's family	
Keila ya alimentó a su gato	Keila already fed her cat	
¿Ya comiste?	Did you already eat?	
¿Ya aprendiste a manejar un auto?	Did you already learn how to drive a car?	
¿Ya sabes hablar otro idioma?	Do you already know how to speak another language?	
¿Ya llegó el profesor?	Did the professor already arrive?	
¿Ya lavaste los platos?	Did you already wash the dishes?	

11.5 Aún

It is a phrase that indicates that an action has not been completed. This type of action can be affirmative or negative. It is also used in the form of a question to find out if an action has been completed. Because this book focuses on the study of basic tenses, the expression "aún"(still) will be explained with expressions of the present type, present in the form of a gerund and past with a gerund in the past (whose expression includes the word "when", with in order to specify an action collateral to that indicated by the phrase "yet").

Observe the following sentences

*Present	
Elías aún no conoce otros lugares	Elías does not know other places yet
Pedro aún está con Luis en la tienda	Pedro is still with Luis at the store
Marcos aún no recuerda quién es su profesor	Marcos does not remember yet who his teacher is

Pablo aún vive en otro continente	Pablo still lives in another continent
Sara no sabe que aún tiene otra oportunidad	Sara does not know that she still has another chance

*Present + gerund	
Patricia aún está conversando con sus colegas	Patricia is still talking with her colleagues
Carlos aún está cuidando el jardín	Carlos is still caring for the garden
Los niños aún no están colaborando con sus padres	The kids are not collaborating with thor parents yet
Gerardo aún no está enviando las cartas correspondientes	Gerard is not sending the corresponding letters yet
¿Aún estás leyendo la misma página?	Are you still reading the same page?
¿Aún estás dudando?	Are you still doubting?

*Past + imperfect + gerund / imperfect+gerund +past	
Cuando el avión llegó, Roberto aún estaba caminando hacia la puerta de embarque.	When the plane arrived, Roberto was still walking to the gate
Pedro aún estaba cocinando cuando su mamá llamó por teléfono	Pedro was still cooking whn his mother called on the phone
Cuando Benjamín tomó el examen, sus amigos aún estaban tomando otra clase	When Benjamin took the exam, his friends were still taking another class
Luis aún estaba caminando hacia el tren cuando este se fue.	Luis was still walking to the train when it left.
Muchos turistas estaban aún visitando la galería cuando comenzó a llover	Many tourists were still visiting the gallery when it began to rain

Practice

Mark with an "A" sentences in active voice and with a "P", sentences in passive voice.

Esa alfombra fue comprada en otro país	That carpet was bought in another country	
Leonardo leyó el libro	Lonardo read the book	
Los poemas fueron escritos por ella	The poems were written by her	
Carlos y su familia visitan los museos mensualmente	Carlos and his family visit the museums monthly	

El auto fue vendido ayer	The car was sold yesterday	

Complete the sentences with "aún" or "ya". Sometimes both words fit.

¿_____ estás trabajando en la empresa?	¿Are you _____ working at the company?
Yo sé que Leonardo _____ terminó su carrera universitaria.	I know Leonardo _____ finished his career.
Teresa _____ está haciendo la tarea.	Teresa is _____ doing the homework.

Write (p/t) if the expression means (period of time, or consequence (c))

Pablo no comió la ensalada. Por eso, quiere comprar una en el restaurante.	Pablo did not eat the salad. That's why, he wants to buy one at the restaurant.	
Carlos quiere ir de vacaciones por un mes.	Carlos wants to go on vacation for a month.	
Luis no asistirá al concierto. Por eso, le dará su ticket a Beatriz.	Luis will not go to the concert. That's why, he will give Beatriz his ticket.	

Complete with the appropriate form of the verb

Esta carta_____escrita por Carlos Come Fue escribe	This letter was written by Carlos
Manuel _____muchas notas Lee Cocina Limpia	Manuel_____many notes

Write "T" if it is grammatically correct or "F" if it is incorrect

¿Ya fuiste a ese país?	
¿Aún comiste mañana?	
¿Tanto ya comes?	

Mark "x" in correct meanings

Elías aún tiene hambre	

Gustavo ya aún tiene hambre	

José ya fue a comprar frutas	
José irá fue a comprar frutas	

Answer keys

Chapter 1:

3.- Arrange the following words to make a question and answer:

*¿Qué día es hoy?
Hoy es miércoles.

4.- From the following sentences, underline the countable nouns.

Peces
Horas
Lápiz

Chapter 2:

*Estoy en el (ordinal number) piso.
*Carlos obtuvo el (ordinal number) lugar.

*Complete the sentences with the appropiate information about family.

(name) es mi papá.
(name) es mi tía.
(name) es mi abuelo.
(name) es mi primo.

Mark with an "x" (in the Spanish box) the appropiate answer.

Tío
Hermana
Hermanos

Complete the sentences with the appropriate form of the verb "ser" related to the time.

Es
Es
Son

Mark with an "x" the correct answer.

Son las 2:00 pm en punto-----x

Faltan 20 para las 3:00 pm-----x

Mark with an "x" the correct expression

¿Qué hora es?------x

Chapter 3

Underline the correct word for each option.

*casa
*jardín
*ventana
*cocina
*lámpara

Choose the correct word to give sense to the sentences

*lámpara
*escalera

Mark with an "x" the correct answer
*elefante
*pez

Mark with an "x" the correct answer.
*perro

Choose the correct word to complete the sentences about transport

*tren
*avión
*auto

Mark with an "x" the correct answer

*estación de tren-------x
*parada de bús--------x

Chapter 4

Complete the following sentences and questions with the appropiate definite or indefinite articles.

*la
*las
*el
*los

¿Un, uno, una, unos? Look at the phrases and fill in the boxes with the best answer.

*unas
*unos
*un
*una

Underline the correct pronoun based on the subjects.

*él
*ellos
*ellas
*nosotros / nosotras
*nosotros / nosotras
*ustedes

Complete the sentences with the appropiate word according to the gender.

*casa
*lámpara

Mark with an "x" the correct demonstrative.

*estos

Choose the right option in the following sentences

*yo
*él

Chapter 5

Match the following ideas to make sense.

Cocinar---en la cocina
Compartir----en el parquet
Aprender----en la escuela

Choose the correct option.

*compra
*aprende

Choose the correct option to make sense.

*en la escuela
*zapatos

Complete with the correct ending form of the verb.

*o
*en

Fill in the space with the correct form

*e
*en

Mark with an "x" the correct option:

*comparte
*comparten

Chapter 6

Complete the spaces with the correct form of the verb "ser"

*es
*son
*somos

Choose the correct answer.

*tiene
*tienen

Mark with an "x" the best option.

*los
*los

Choose the correct answer.

*siempre
*martes

Fill in with the correct answer.

*hago
*hacen

Choose the correct form

*juega
*juegan

Chapter 7

Choose the correct word; ¿cuánto?, ¿cuánta?, ¿cuántos?, ¿cuántas?

*cuánto
*cuántas
*cuántos
*cuánta

Read the conversation. Underline possessive adjectives.

1º sentence: su
7º sentence: mis

Match the correct option.

*mí
*les

Choose the correct form
*está
*están

Choose the correct form of possessive adjectives.
*mi
*nuestra

Chapter 8

Observe the expressions.

*Read the dialogue between Rodrigo and a taxi driver.
*Observe another type of dialogue.
*Read the questions. Observe different questions beginning with question words and some beginning with verbs. Mark with an "x" the ones beginning with question words.

*¿Cuándo?
*¿Por qué?
*¿A qué hora?
*¿Qué?

Match the phrases to give meaning.

*¿Dónde queda------el cine?
*¿Cuándo es ------tu cumpleaños?
*¿Te gusta-----la ciudad?

Mark with an "x" the correct complement.

*siempre
*la

Chapter 9

Observe the two columns. Match actions coherently.

*¿Dónde están comiendo------Elisa y John?
*¿Quién está estudiando-----con Martha?
*¿Por qué estás-------------estudiando ahora?
*¿Cómo estás----------cocinando?

Read the following recipe.

Read the following sentences about preterite imperfect + gerund. Underline the verbs in this form.

*estaba jugando
*estaba cocinando
*estaban escuchando
*estaban comiendo
*estaban Miguel y su familia limpiando

Match the sentences to give the correct meaning.

*¿Por qué--------estabas comiendo ayer en el restaurante?

*¿Cuándo-------estabas en el restaurante?

*¿A quién-----------le gusta añadir ingredientes a la limonada?

Match the phrases with the correct form.

*¿Los profesores-------------comieron en la escuela?

*¿Preparaste la ensalada--------ayer?

Read the verbs (infinitive form) with their past forms.

Write "T" for true and "F" for false.

*T
*F
*T
*F

Chapter 10

From the second column, write "T" for tru conditional forms and "F" for false conditional forms.

*F
*T
*F
*T

Underline the verbal periphrasis "ir a " conjugated.

*van a
*van a
*va a

Match the correct phrases in Spanish.

*Pablo piensa que -----la casa es muy grande.
*Ellos piensan que------María es su nueva profesora.
*Nosotros---------pensamos que tus notas son muy buenas.
*¿Ustedes pensaron---------que ellos son muy felices?

Write "T" if the sentence is correct, "F" for if it is incorrect.

*Carla supo manejar el auto-----"T"

Mark "x" in the correct sentence

*¿Quieres tomar jugo?

Complete the sentences with the correct form of the verb.

*trabajará

Chapter 11

Mark with an "A" sentences in active voice and with a "P", sentences in passive voice.

*P
*A
*P

*A
*P

Complete the sentences with "aún" or "ya". Sometimes both words fit.

*aún
*ya
*aún

Write (p/t) if the expression means period of time, or (c) if the expression means consequence.

*c
*p/t
*c

Complete with the appropriate form of the verbs.

*fue
*lee

Write "T" if it is grammatically correct or "F" if it is incorrect.

*T
*F
*F

Mark "x" in correct meanings.

Elías aún tiene hambre------x

Spanish Phrasebook For

Beginners

Learn Common Phrases In Context With
Explanations For Everyday Use and Travel

Worldwide Nomad

Introduction

In the intricate mosaic of languages spoken worldwide, few are as alluring, mysterious, and above all, useful as the Spanish language. With its rhythmic cadence, elegant structure, and diverse cultural heritage, Spanish stands not just as a means of communication but as a gateway to understanding a nation deeply rooted in tradition and innovation.

Welcome to *Learn Conversational Spanish,* a journey through the heart and soul of this extraordinary language. Whether you're an aspiring traveler, a business professional eager to broaden your horizons, or simply someone captivated by the beauty of Spanish culture, this book is your key to unlocking the door to speaking and understanding conversational Spanish.

This book is crafted with the aim of empowering you with essential skills and knowledge to engage in meaningful conversations in Spanish. It caters to learners of all levels, from absolute beginners to those looking to enhance their existing Spanish language skills. By the end of this book, you will not only have a solid grasp of conversational Spanish but also a deeper appreciation for Spanish culture and customs.

Have you ever envisioned strolling through the charming streets of Barcelona, Mexico City, Bogota, Buenos Aires, San Salvador, Lima or Santiago? Have you ever dreamed of immersing yourself in the rich cultural history of the Hispanic world? Conversational Spanish is your passport to such experiences. This book is purposefully designed.

First and foremost, it seeks to equip you with practical communication skills. Whether you find yourself ordering your favorite Spanish dish at a local restaurant, seeking directions, or engaging in casual banter with locals, this book provides you with the ability to communicate effectively in everyday situations.

Secondly, this book offers cultural insights. It delves into the intricacies of Spanish culture, values, and customs, enriching your interactions and fostering meaningful connections with native speakers. Understanding the cultural context of the language will not only enhance your proficiency but also deepen your appreciation of Spanish culture.

This book is also tailored to boost your confidence in speaking Spanish. It achieves this by gradually introducing you to the language's fundamentals and guiding you through practical exercises and real-life dialogues. As you progress through the chapters, you will find yourself becoming more comfortable and proficient in expressing yourself in Spanish.

When it comes to Spanish, a language renowned for its beauty and global influence, the initial intimidation can be overwhelming. However, fear not—this book is meticulously written to transform your language-learning journey into an enjoyable and highly effective experience.

In addition to linguistic proficiency, we will offer invaluable cultural insights. By exploring the customs, traditions, and etiquette that shape both the language and its native speakers, you will gain a deeper appreciation of Spanish culture. This cultural understanding will not only enrich your interactions but also foster a sense of respect and connection with the people you communicate with.

The ability to navigate real-life scenarios is an essential component of language learning. This book equips you with the necessary tools to excel in practical situations by providing dialogues and vocabulary tailored to everyday conversations. Whether you're ordering your favorite Spanish dish at a restaurant or seeking directions on the bustling streets of Spain, you'll be well-prepared for your interactions, ensuring that your experiences in Spain are both enjoyable and enriching.

Now that you possess the essential linguistic tools from the Spanish Grammar book, it's time to apply them to real-world situations. From ordering delectable dishes at a local restaurant to seeking directions through unfamiliar streets and engaging in casual chit-chat, we will prepare you for the myriad of everyday scenarios you may encounter while exploring Spain.

Language and culture are inextricably intertwined, forming the essence of a nation's identity. You'll gain profound insights into Spanish customs, traditions, and social etiquette. This cultural understanding ensures that your conversations not only maintain linguistic accuracy but also reflect a deep respect for the rich tapestry of Spanish culture.

Building upon the sturdy foundation established earlier, you'll be introduced to an expansive array of vocabulary. You'll acquire words and phrases spanning various topics, empowering you to engage in diverse conversations and express your thoughts and emotions with precision.

Throughout this book, you'll find that the Spanish language is not just a means of communication; it's a key that opens doors to a rich and vibrant culture. So, let's embark on this adventure together. Ready your Spanish alphabet characters, sharpen your curiosity, and let's set sail into the world of Conversational Spanish!

Chapter 1
Counting in Spanish

In the vibrant tapestry of the Spanish language, mastering numbers is a key that opens doors to seamless communication and practical interactions. In this guide, we'll embark on a journey to demystify the realm of numbers in conversational Spanish. From the basics of counting to navigating everyday scenarios involving prices, payments, and more, let's dive into the fascinating world where numbers come alive.

Numbers serve as the cornerstone of language, and even know we rarely notice in our native languages, they play an indispensable role in our daily interactions. Almost every sentence spoken or written has a numeric expression. We usc numbers in situations that range from merely counting to telling time, expressing quantities, and discussing prices. We have decided to start off this book with this essential part because a strong command of numbers and money-related vocabulary can empower you to have effective communication in your Spanish journey.

Whether you're embarking on a shopping spree in lively markets, indulging in the culinary delights of local restaurants, or simply engaging in conversations with Spanish-speaking friends from Latin America or Spain, a solid understanding of numbers and currency will significantly enhance your ability to connect.

Let's begin by immersing ourselves in the Spanish number system. Our initial focus will be on comprehending how to count, tell time, and express dates in a way that aligns with the rich Hispanic cultural context. Once we've established a firm foundation in numbers, we'll venture into the enchanting world of money. In this exploration, we'll learn how to discuss prices, conduct transactions, and navigate financial exchanges with confidence.

You'll uncover key vocabulary and phrases that empower you to shop effortlessly, negotiate skillfully, and manage your finances seamlessly within Spanish-speaking environments. Our approach here involves providing clear explanations and practical examples to reinforce your learning. It's crucial to recognize that mastering numbers and money in Spanish isn't solely about acquiring language skills but also about gaining cultural insights.

These insights will not only enhance your experiences in Latin America and with Hispanic communities worldwide but also deepen your appreciation for the unique aspects of their vibrant cultures. By the end of this journey, you'll be well-equipped to handle everyday situations with confidence and ease. Your enhanced language proficiency and cultural appreciation will contribute to a more fulfilling and enjoyable exploration of life in the Hispanic world. ¡Vamos a empezar! (Let's get started!)

Numbers and money are integral aspects of our daily lives, and delving into their understanding is key to unlocking the richness of your experiences in Spanish-speaking regions. Whether you're reveling in the vibrant markets in South America, or savoring the flavors of local cuisine in Mexico, or connecting with friends the lovely people of Central America, mastering the nuances of numbers and money is your passport to fully enjoying life in the Hispanic world. Let's delve into why acquiring these skills is not just practical but also an exciting gateway to the diverse and lively cultures that await you.

Getting Started: Numbers 1-20

Before delving into the intricacies, let's start with the foundation. Familiarize yourself with the numbers from 1 to 20, as they lay the groundwork for more complex expressions. Practice counting and recognize their pronunciation, a skill essential for any Spanish learner.

(1) Uno – one

(2) Dos – two

(3) Tres – three

(4) Cuatro – four

(5) Cinco – five

(6) Seis – six

(7) Siete – seven

(8) Ocho – eight

(9) Nueve – nine

(10) Diez – ten

(11) Once – eleven

(12) Doce – twelve

(13) Trece – thirteen

(14) Catorce – fourteen

(15) Quince – fifteen

(16) Dieciséis – sixteen

(17) Diecisiete – seventeen

(18) Dieciocho – eighteen

(19) Diecinueve – nineteen

(20) Veinte - twenty

For the most part, numbers in Spanish are easy to learn once you are familiar with the patterns. However, numbers 11 *once* to 15 *quince* in Spanish pose a unique challenge for learners due to their irregularities compared to the pattern observed in the rest of the counting sequence. While numbers from 16 onward in Spanish follow a more straightforward structure, the transitional phase from 10 *diez* to 15 *quince* introduces alterations that demand special attention.

The presence of irregularities, such as 11 *once* and 12 *doce*, deviating from the conventional ten plus unit format that is followed in the rest of the numbers as you will see below, can be initially perplexing. Additionally, the pronunciation nuances, especially with numbers like 14 *catorce* and 15 *quince*, further contribute to the complexity.

The irregularities in this range underscore the importance of focused practice and repetition to solidify these foundational numbers in the learning process. Do not be scared or frustrated though. Once a learner overcomes this obstacle, counting in Spanish is one of the easiest elements in mastering the language.

Tens and Beyond: Numbers 20-100

Let's explore the structure of larger numbers, from 20 *veinte* to 100 *cien*. We will learn how to compose these numbers and understand the pattern they follow. This section will equip you to express a wide range of quantities, crucial for day-to-day conversations.

Since we have covered the numbers from 1 *uno* to 20 *veinte*. Let's move forwards and see how the tens work in Spanish.

> (21) Veintiuno
> (22) Veintidós
> (23) Veintitrés
> (24) Veinticuatro
> (25) Veinticinco
> (26) Veintiséis
> (27) Veintisiete
> (28) Veintiocho
> (29) Veintinueve
> (30) Treinta

The remaining tens up to one hundred are as follows:

> (40) Cuarenta
> (50) Cincuenta
> (60) Sesenta
> (70) Setenta
> (80) Ochenta
> (90) Noventa
> (100) Cien

From 30 *treinta* on, we only need to add the conjunction "*y*" and the unit to make up the rest of the numbers.

For example, 31 would be: *treinta y uno.*
32 *treinta y dos;*
44 *cuarenta y cuatro;*
57 *cincuenta y siete;*
63 *sesenta y tres;*
79 *setenta y nueve;*
81 *ochenta y uno;*
92 *noventa y dos.*

100 and Beyond

Now that you've learned how to form the Spanish numbers from 1 to 99, let's move on to the larger figures. To do this we will learn the number 100 and the multiples of 1000. Once you master this, it is only a matter of combining the numbers from 1-99 with the hundreds and thousands to create bigger numbers.

100 *cien*
From 101 on, you do not use *cien*. Instead, you use *ciento*.

Thus:
101 *ciento uno*
115 *ciento quince*
136 *ciento treinta y seis*
199 *ciento noventa y nueve*
200 *doscientos*
300 *trescientos*
400 *cuatrocientos*

500 *quinientos* – Pay special attention here as it is the only number in the hundreds that is irregular, that is, it does not follow the pattern. It is common to hear Spanish learners to say *"cincocientos"*. This mistake is common even in advanced learners. You have to know that locals will understand what you mean, but it is not the correct way to say this number.

600 *seiscientos*
700 *setecientos*
800 *ochocientos*
900 novecientos
1000 *mil*

In Spanish, the terms setecientos and novecientos deviate from the expected patterns of sietecientos and nuevecientos. This linguistic divergence is rooted in historical and phonetic considerations, as they come from Latin numbers 7 septem and 9 novem. In the case of setecientos, the insertion of the vowel "e" serves to enhance the fluidity of pronunciation. Similarly, novecientos includes the vowel "o" for phonetic convenience.

Decimals

Decimals are easy to learn in Spanish. You only need to express the units and the decimals with the numbers we have just learned. If you are in a market, or restaurant, or just buying some souvenirs from a small store, you will most likely be told:

El precio es quince cincuenta (15.50).

The price is 15.50.
or
Cuesta veinticinco noventa (25.90).

It is 25.90.

Get familiar with the currency of the countries you plan to visit or live in. Countries like Panama, Ecuador and El Salvador use American Dollars as legal tender. The rest of the countries use different currencies, and the exchange rate are different from country to county.

One dollar can be 17 Mexican Pesos, but if you are in Colombia, it is 4050 Colombian Pesos. In Costa Rica, one dollar is equal a 530 Colones, and in Peru the exchange rate is $1 to 3.77 Soles.

If what you are expressing is mathematical ciphers, add the word "punto" the unites and the decimals.

So, 15.50 will be: *quince punto cincuenta.*

By extending your numerical understanding of decimals, you can easily grasp the concepts required to express quantities or dealing with measurements. mastering these nuances will enhance your ability to navigate various contexts with ease.

Market Conversations - Asking for Prices

Equip yourself with the necessary vocabulary to navigate a bustling *mercado*. Learn how to ask for prices, quantities, and express preferences. A practical approach to language ensures a seamless shopping experience.

The basic expressions in these circumstances are:

¿Cuánto cuesta? – How much is it?

This expression is used when you see or find something you are/might be interested in.

¿Cuánto le debo? – How much do I owe you?

This expression is used when you are at the counter or in front of the cashier/seller and you are about to pay.

¿Puede darme un precio más bajo? – Can you give me a lower price?

This is the common expression when bargaining or trying to get a lower price for a product you really want to buy but you think that the seller might accept a lower price, or they are trying to charge more than what it really costs.

Handling Money

Before delving into the nuances of handling money, courtesy, credit cards and avoiding scams in Latin America and Spain, it's essential to acquaint yourself with the local currencies:

Mexico: Peso mexicano
Guatemala: Quetzal
El Salvador: Dólar americano
Honduras: Lempira
Nicaragua: Córdoba
Costa Rica: Colón
Panama: Balboa / Dólar americano
Colombia: Peso colombiano
Peru: Sol
Ecuador: Dólar americano
Chile: Peso chileno
Argentina: Peso argentino
Paraguay: Guaraní
Uruguay: Peso uruguayo
Venezuela: Bolivar
Spain: Euro

Useful Vocabulary

Bill (bandknote): Billete
Coin: Moneda
Currency Exchange rate: Tasa de cambio or tipo de cambio
Check: Cheque
Bank: Banco
Transaction: Transacción

If, for example, you want to exchange some money in your destination country, some phrase that you might find extremely useful are:

Me gustaría cambiar $1000 (mil dólares) a pesos colombianos.

I'd like to exchange $1000 for Colombian Pesos.

¿Cuál es la tasa de cambio?

What is the exchange rate?

¿Dónde puedo cambiar dólares por soles?

Where can I exchange dollars for soles?

Usually, people working at the money exchange locations are mandated to ask for a personal ID, so be ready to answer the following questions:

¿Podría mostrarme una identificación o pasaporte?

Could you show me an ID or passport?

Necesito ver una identificación o pasaporte?

I need to see an ID or passport.

Then you need to answer: *¡Aquí tiene!* Which translates as "Here you have!"

Navigating Transactions with Credit Cards

Credit and debit cards are widely accepted, but it's advisable to carry some cash for smaller purchases or for use in places that do not accept cards. Credit cards are widely accepted in every Hispanic country, but it's a good practice to check whether there are any surcharges for using a credit card, especially for small purchases. Some businesses may prefer cash for smaller transactions.

If you are using public transportation, make sure you always have cash, and it is even better if you have the exact amount of money to pay for each trip.

Unfortunately, Latin American countries are still new to adopting digital payments through digital wallets that you can use in your phones or smart watches. If you are planning on traveling or moving soon to one of these countries, you might have to wait a little longer for these services to become common. The only exception to this rule is Spain.

Paying and Receiving the Change

When you pay with money, be patient. The cashier or the person assisting you will count the money in front of you. This could be done even twice or three times if the amount of money is considerable ($50 dollars or above or the equivalent in the local currency).

When they handle back the change to you, the cashier or server will wait and will expect you to count to change to verify that you have received the exact amount. You are expected to at least take a look at the banknotes or coins and acknowledge that everything is correct by saying:

Todo está perfecto or *El cambio está bien.*

Everything is perfect or The change is correct.

Conclusion

Understanding the local traditions and views of money, service charges, and additional fees will help you manage your budget effectively and make informed financial choices during your trip in the Hispanic world.

Now you've explored a diverse array of topics, from learning about the different currencies and mastering the art of negotiation to comprehending tipping customs and embracing money-saving strategies. We are sure now you have a good understanding of how to pay, what to say, and what to expect when completing a transaction in Spanish.

As we conclude, it's vital to recognize that these skills not only serve practical purposes but also serve as cultural bridges, facilitating deeper connections and meaningful interactions. These newly acquired abilities will not only enhance your financial acumen but also enrich your engagement with the local cultures.

As you continue your journey to learn conversational Spanish, always remember that practice and immersion are key to mastery in these essential facets of language and culture.

Now, for Chapter 2, it's time for you to learn how to greet others warmly, navigate social customs gracefully, and introduce yourself confidently. These skills will not only help you initiate conversations but also foster positive connections with locals.

Chapter 2
Greeting in Spanish

The Basics

Introducing yourself in a Latin American or Hispanic country involves expressing warmth, friendliness, and a genuine interest in building connections. Unlike North American or most European countries, Hispanic people are open to get to know others, and they will treat you as a friend since the very beginning.

Here's a small guide to help you navigate introductions in a Latin American and Hispanic settings as well as the most useful phrase you will need to establish a good first conversation:

Start with a Greeting

Begin with a friendly greeting. Whether you are greeting a friend or someone you see for the first time, the first greeting has to be warm and friendly. Your energy when greeting will determine the rest of the of the conversation.

So, if you are here to make friends, do not be shy.

In many Spanish speaking countries, people often use hugs or kisses on the cheek, especially among friends and acquaintances. Handshakes are also common in more formal settings, but the level of physical contact may seem to be uncomfortable at the beginning and may vary by region and individual preferences. However, you will soon start liking greeting people like this. There is nothing as to be received with a hug!

Use Formal Titles

If you're in a formal setting, address people using their titles and last names until given permission to use first names. "Señor" (Mr.) and "Señora" (Mrs.) are commonly used titles before the person's last name.

Some formal greetings are:
Buenos días, señor López
Good morning, Mr. Lopez
Buenas tardes, señora García.
Good afternoon, Mrs. Gracia
¡Qué gusto saludarlos, señores Martínez!
Very pleased to greet you, Mr. and Mrs. Martinez!

Express Politeness

Do not forget about politeness. Despite people being physical and hugging and kissing in the cheeks to greet you, politeness and manners are still highly valued. Respect personal space, let the elder speak first, do not interrupt someone when they are speaking, and always, ALWAYS, use polite expressions like *por favor* (please) and *gracias* (thank you) frequently.

If you are eating at a table, always ask for permission to:

1. Have more food or drinks:

¿Puedo tomar más pollo/limonada/ensalada/arroz?

Can I have more chicken/lemonade/salad/rice?

2. Leave the table:

¿Me disculpan? Necesito ir al baño/atender esta llamada.

Can you excuse me? I need to go to the restroom/answer this call.

3. Interrupt the person speaking:

¿Puedo decir algo? or *Me gustaría decir algo.*

Can I say something? or I'd like to say something.

(Do not) Be Mindful of Time

Latin American cultures often have a more relaxed attitude toward time. Don't be overly concerned about punctuality and expect conversations to take their natural course. If a conversation is flowing and you are the guest, do not end the conversation abruptly.

Instead, let your hosts or the other people when you need to leave in advance so that they are aware of your time constraints.

It is recommended that you mention something like:

Necesito irme en 30 minutos para alcanzar mi bus.

I need to leave in 30 minutes to catch my bus.

Me *tengo que ir a mi hotel/casa en 30 minutos para descansar.*

I have to go to my hotel/house to rest.

Know that giving a 30-minute notice is considered the best way to announce that you cannot stay longer. Also know that if an event is scheduled at a certain time, the most likely scenario is that people will start showing up 30 to 45 minutes later than the established time. Being punctual is not a thing in Hispanic countries and all people are aware of this.

Hands and Arms

Do not be afraid to use gestures when being in a Spanish speaking country. You will soon notice that locals use gestures for everything, especially when giving examples and talking about distances or sizes.

People from some cultures keep their hands and arms to their side and use them in limited ways. This is not the case for Hispanic people. Gestures and movements enrich the conversations and make them more vivid! Of course, do not forget to respect others' personal space!

Engage in Small Talk

Small talk may be very superficial in some cultures, but in the Hispanic world, it is a great way to break the ice. If you ask someone how they are doing, do not expect to hear a simple "nice" as an answer. If you ask or are asked how your day is going, that is a signal to establish a conversation. Responding *"bien"* and continue your way will be considered disrespectful.

If you want to start a conversation or begin a friendship with someone new, ask about the other person's day, family, or interests. Common topics include family, sports, and local culture. People will not respond briefly. Hispanic people are passionate about these topics, and they will openly talk about them.

Some useful phrases are:
¿Cómo *está?* (formal)
¿Cómo *estás?* (informal)
How are you?
¿Cómo estuvo su fin de semana? (formal)
¿Cómo estuvo tu fin de semana? *(informal)*
How was your weekend?
¿Cómo está *su familia?* (formal)
¿Cómo está *tu familia?* (informal)

How is your family doing?
¿Qué le gusta hacer en su tiempo libre? (formal)
¿Qué *te gusta hacer en tu tiempo libre? (informal)*
What do you like doing in your free time?

Use Formal Language

As we saw in the previous questions, there is a formal and an informal way to treat others. The formal way is using the pronoun *usted* which uses the same verb conjugation as the pronouns *he* and *she.*

The informal way uses the pronouns *tú* and *vos* (in Argentina, Uruguay, Paraguay and in El Salvador). These pronouns use the same verb conjugation. The only difference is with the verb **ser**. In these conjugations, *vos* uses the conjugation form *sos,* and *tú* uses the regular form eres.

Vos sos mi mejor amigo.
Tú eres mi mejor amigo.
You are my best friend.
For the rest of the verbs, the conjugation is the same.
Tú estás aquí / Vos estás aquí.
You are here.
Tú trabajas en la escuela / Vos trabajás en la escuela.
You work in the school.

Until you are familiar with the level of formality in a particular setting, it's advisable to use formal language, that is, using *usted* to address others. This is especially true when addressing older individuals or those in positions of authority.

Once you have gained others' trust, they will start using the *tú/vos* pronouns, and they will also ask you to do the same in the linguistic process known as *tutear* or *vosear.*

Learn Basic Phrases in Spanish

While many Latin Americans speak English, making an effort to communicate in Spanish will be always be appreciated. If people notice you are trying to use Spanish, they will help you, correct you and teach you. It is like having free Spanish lessons every time you speak.

Show Genuine Interest

People in Latin American cultures appreciate genuine interest and curiosity. Ask open-ended questions and actively listen to the responses. As we mentioned before, there is no such a thing like small talk in Spanish speaking countries. If you start a conversation, be ready to engage in the conversation for a while.

Participate in Cultural Customs

If there are specific cultural customs or traditions, try to participate. In fact, locals will expect you to participate and even volunteer for whatever activity that is taking place. Whether it's sharing a traditional meal or attending local events or even a dance, involvement fosters a sense of connection.

Though they will not feel offended if you say no, do not skip these opportunities to engage and show others that you are there to enjoy, learn and have a terrific time!

Remember, every country and region within Latin America has its own unique customs and nuances, so it's essential to be adaptable and observant. The key is to approach introductions with respect, an open mind, and a willingness to embrace the local culture.

Chapter 3
Transportation

ow, it is time to learn about useful words and phrases that every traveler will need in their trip through Latin America and Spain. Let's embark on a linguistic journey through the vibrant and dynamic world of transportation with this chapter. We will delve into the rich tapestry of the Spanish language, unraveling the common phrases that seamlessly weave through the daily experiences of moving from one place to another.

These phrases will help you navigate with ease every corner of Latin America and Spain, from bustling city streets to tranquil rural roads. By learning them, you will be able to talk to locals, ask for help and directions, ask for bus, train, or metro fares, and enjoy your rides even more.

You should be aware that transportation in Hispanic countries reflects not only their means of getting around but also the cultural nuances that shape their sociological and economical perspectives.

As we navigate the linguistic landscape, we will encounter phrases that capture the essence of travel, offering insights into the customs, habits, and attitudes surrounding transportation in Spanish-speaking regions. Whether you are a language enthusiast, a traveler eager to connect with locals, or simply curious about the idiomatic expressions that color everyday conversations, this chapter will invite you to explore the linguistic crossroads where language and transportation intersect.

Ready for this trip? Join us in this linguistic excursion as we unravel the meanings behind phrases that transcend mere words, painting vivid pictures of the diverse modes of transportation and the unique ways in which they are embedded in the Spanish-speaking world. From the rhythmic cadence of urban commutes to the leisurely pace of rural travels, each phrase is a snapshot of the cultural landscapes that shape the Spanish language.

So, fasten your seatbelt, hop on board, and let us be your passport to the captivating world of transportation idioms in Spanish. Through the lens of language, we embark on a fascinating exploration of the expressions that bridge the gap between where we are and where we want to go.

Before we move on to the phrases and vocabulary, here you have some piece of information that will be worthy.

Buses

The bus systems in Latin America form a dynamic and integral part of daily life, reflecting the region's diverse cultures, landscapes, and urban structures. Buses are used by everyone, and they are not only a way of transport, but also a place to meet locals and have awesome conversations.

If you spend more than a couple of days in one city and you use the public transportation frequently enough, you will notice how the bus drivers recognize you and show genuine happiness every time you get on the bus. They will soon learn the places that you visit the most and the bus stops when you get off. People will also greet you and some will even start off a conversation, so be ready to talk and do not be scared! It is common to talk to the person next to you when traveling in a bus.

Buses are unique. Latin American cities are characterized by a colorful array of buses navigating through bustling streets and winding mountainous roads, these systems cater to the transportation needs of millions. In many Latin American cities, buses operate on extensive networks, connecting neighborhoods, suburbs, and even remote areas, providing a lifeline for those who rely on public transportation.

The bus routes are often intricate, adapting to the unique topography and urban layouts, and passengers experience a vibrant mosaic of local life as they traverse through diverse communities. While some cities boast modern, organized systems, others showcase a more informal yet effective approach, where buses operate independently or within loosely regulated frameworks. You will surely have to ask a local: ¿*Cada cuánto pasa el bus?* which translates as how frequent are the buses?

Some buses are extremely frequent, for example, every 3 minutes. Others, depending on the final destination, might take from 15 to 40 minutes. If you are early or miss the bus, do not panic. Some more people will join you at the bus stop and you will have enough time to talk about the city, the people, your destination, politics… whatever you feel like talking. Bus stops are, in fact, places to gather and have social interactions while waiting.

Regarding fares, the affordability and accessibility of buses make them a popular mode of transportation, fostering a sense of community among passengers who share the journey amidst the rhythmic hum of engines and the lively chatter of diverse voices. The bus systems in Latin America thus embody not only the practicality of transit but also the cultural tapestry that binds the region together.

As we mentioned in the previous chapter, the best practice is to have the exact fare every time you pay for your ride. If you pay with a banknote and the driver does not have enough change, you will have to wait until more people pay and driver has enough coins or small bills to charge you and give you your change. This might take a couple of bus stops and even the whole ride, from bus terminal to bus terminal.

Metros and Subways

In Latin America and the biggest and important cities in Spain, several cities boast efficient and extensive metro systems, representing a modern and organized approach to urban transportation. These metros serve as the arterial veins of bustling metropolises, navigating through the complex networks of sprawling urban landscapes. Spanish speaking cities like Barcelona, Madrid, Panama City, Mexico City, and Buenos Aires (Subte) brag about having clean and punctual metro systems.

Designed to alleviate traffic congestion and provide a rapid means of transit, these metro systems cater to the diverse needs of their urban populations. The make use of well-maintained stations, which also serve as dynamic museums often decorated with pieces of arts or adorned with unique architectural features.

It is not a secret that the metro systems in Latin America and Spain showcase a commitment to both functionality and aesthetics. Passengers experience a seamless journey, with trains connecting key destinations across the city, making the metro an integral part of daily life for millions.

These underground arteries not only efficiently transport people but also contribute to the cultural and economic vibrancy of the cities they serve, embodying a modern, forward-thinking approach to urban mobility in Latin America.

Taxis and Ride-Sharing Services

Finally, taxis and ride-sharing services, such as Uber or Lyft, play a crucial role in the transportation landscape of Latin America, offering a flexible and convenient alternative for both locals and visitors. In many cities across the region, taxis are readily available, identifiable by their distinctive colors and signage (pink and white in Mexico City, Red in Costa Rica, and the typical yellow and black in the rest of the countries).

They weave through the bustling streets as integral components of the urban fabric. These traditional taxis often operate on metered systems, providing passengers with a transparent and regulated fare structure.

On the other hand, the rise of ride-sharing platforms like Uber has introduced a new dimension to transportation in Latin America. Offering a user-friendly interface and often a cashless payment system, services like Uber and Lyft, or more local services provide a modern and reliable option for getting around. Both traditional taxis and ride-sharing services contribute to the accessibility and efficiency of transportation in Latin America, catering to diverse preferences and contributing to the vibrant mosaic of urban mobility in the region.

Common Phrases and Vocabulary

Common Phrases	Translation
What bus route takes me to …?	¿Qué ruta de bus me lleva a …?
What metro line takes me to …?	¿Qué línea de metro me lleva a …?
How frequent is the bus?	¿Cada cuánto pasa el bus?
How frequent is the train/metro/subte?	¿Cada cuánto pasa el tren/metro/subte?
How much is the bus fare?	¿Cuánto cuesta el bus?
How much is the taxi fare?	¿Cuánto cuesta el taxi?
How much is the metro fare?	¿Cuánto cuesta el metro?
How much is the train fare?	¿Cuánto cuesta el tren?
I need help.	Necesito ayuda.

Where can I take the bus/metro/train/taxi?	¿Dónde puedo tomar el bus/metro/tren/taxi?
Where can I buy a card for the bus/metro/train?	¿Dónde puedo comprar una tarjeta para el bus/metro/tren?
I want to add credit to my card.	Quiero agregar crédito a mi tarjeta.
Where do I have to get off if I need to go to …?	¿Dónde puedo bajarme si necesito ir a …?
What is the closest station?	¿Cuál es la estación más cercana?
Where do I need to transfer?	¿Dónde necesito transbordar?
Where can I transfer?	¿Dónde puedo transbordar?
What time does the bus service begin?	¿A qué hora comienza el servicio de buses?
What time does the bus service finish?	¿A qué hora termina el servicio de buses?
Could you tell me how to get to …?	¿Podría decirme cómo llegar a …?
Am I close to …?	¿Estoy cerca de …?
Can I sit here?	¿Puedo sentarme aquí?
Yes, of course!	Sí, claro.
No, it is taken.	No, está ocupado.
Where is the hospital?	¿Dónde está el hospital?
I need to go to a hospital.	Necesito ir a un hospital.
Where is the police station?	¿Dónde está la estación de policía?
Where do I exit the station?	¿Dónde está la salida de la estación?
What platform do I need if I am going to …?	¿Qué plataforma necesito para ir a …?
Where can I get a map of the metro lines?	¿Dónde puedo conseguir un mapa de las líneas de metro?
Where can I get a map of the bus lines?	¿Dónde puedo conseguir un mapa de las líneas de buses?
Where is the restroom?	¿Dónde está el baño?
How long does the bus take to get to …?	¿Cuánto tiempo tarda el bus en llegar a …?
How long does the train take to get to …?	¿Cuánto tiempo tarda el tren en llegar a …?
How long does the metro take to get to …?	¿Cuánto tiempo tarda el metro en llegar a …?
Can I get there by walking?	¿Puedo ir caminando?
What route is this bus?	¿Qué ruta es este bus?
What line is this train?	¿Qué línea es este tren?
What time is it?	¿Qué hora es?
What time will we arrive?	¿A qué hora llegaremos?
Where can I buy one ticket?	¿Dónde puedo comprar un boleto?
Can I pay with spare money or do I need to buy a card?	¿Puedo pagar con monedas o necesito una tarjeta?

Can I buy a weekly/monthly/unlimited pass?	¿Puedo comprar un pase semanal/mensual/ilimitado?
Is there a student discount?	¿Hay descuento para estudiantes?
Where can I find an available taxi?	¿Dónde puedo encontrar un taxi disponible?
Where is the taxi terminal?	¿Dónde está la terminal de taxis?
Where are you going?	¿Hacia dónde va?
What is your destination?	¿Cuál es su destino?
Please, take me to [location].	Por favor, lléveme a …
I need to go to [location].	Necesito ir a …
How long will it take to get to [location]?	¿Cuánto tiempo tarda en llegar a …?
What is the fare for a trip to [location]?	¿Cuál es el precio de un viaje a …?
Can you drive faster?	¿Puede conducir un poco más rápido?
Can you drive slower?	¿Puede conducir un poco más lento?
Can you turn up volume?	¿Puede subir el volumen?
Can you turn down volume?	¿Puede bajar el volumen?
Can you change the radio station?	¿Puede cambiar la estación de radio?
Can you turn on the radio?	¿Puede encender la radio?
Can you turn off the radio?	¿Puede apagar la radio?
Is it difficult to catch a taxi in this part of the city?	¿Es difícil conseguir un taxi en esta parte de la ciudad?
There is a lot of traffic.	Hay mucho tráfico.
Can I pay with a card or cash?	¿Puedo pagar con tarjeta o con efectivo?
Please, take this route.	Por favor, tome esta ruta.
Please, use the GPS.	Por favor, use el GPS.
Please, open the window.	Por favor, abra la ventana.
Please, close the window.	Por favor, cierre la ventana.
Can you help me with my luggage?	¿Puede ayudarme con mi equipaje?
Can you turn on the AC?	¿Puede encender el aire acondicionado?
Can you turn off the AC?	¿Puede apagar el aire acondicionado?
Please, open the trunk.	¿Puede abrir el maletero/la cajuela?
I'll pay with a card.	Pagaré con una tarjeta.
I'll pay with cash.	Pagaré con efectivo.
You can drop me off here.	Puede dejarme aquí.
You can drop me off there.	Puede bajarme allí.
You can drop me off in the corner.	Puede bajarme en la esquina.
I would like to go to the airport.	Me gustaría ir al aeropuerto.
I would like to go to the museum.	Me gustaría ir al museo.

I would like to go to downtown.	Me gustaría ir al centro de la ciudad.
I would like to go to the hotel …	Me gustaría ir al hotel …
I'll get off here.	Me bajaré aquí.
I'm sorry, can you wait for me a couple of minutes?	Lo siento, ¿puede esperarme unos minutos?
How long will it take to get to my destination?	¿Cuánto tardará en llegar a mi destino?
How can I get to [location] from here?	¿Cómo puedo llegar a … desde aquí?
What time is rush hour?	¿A qué hora es la hora pico?
Can I have your card for future trips?	¿Me puede dar su tarjeta para futuros viajes?
Can you stop by the supermarket on the way back?	¿Puede parar en el supermercado en el camino de regreso?
How long have you been a driver and what places do you recommend in the city?	¿Cuánto tiempo ha sido un conductor y qué lugares recomienda visitar?
Is this part of the city safe?	¿Esta parte de la ciudad es segura?
Until what time do you operate?	¿Hasta qué hora trabajan?
Let me know when I can get off.	Dígame cuando pueda bajarme.
Do you have a phone charger?	¿Tiene un cargador de teléfono?
Please, take me to the downtown area.	Por favor, lléveme al centro de la ciudad.
Please, take me to the downtown bus terminal.	Por favor, lléveme a la terminal de buses del centro.
Please, stop at the next gas station.	Por favor, pare en la siguiente gasolinera.
I can walk from here.	Puedo caminar desde aquí.
Thank you for bringing me home.	Gracias por traerme a casa.
Have a nice day/evening/night.	Tenga un buen día/buena tarde/buena noche.

Vocabulary	Translation
Good morning!	¡Buenos días!
Good afternoon!	¡Buenas tardes!
Good evening! Good night!	¡Buenas noches!
Metro/train station	Estación de metro/tren
Metro/train Terminal	Terminal de metro/tren
Fare	Tarifa
Map	Mapa
Transfers	Transbordos
Departures	Salidas
Arrivals	Llegadas
Schedule	Horario

Restroom	Baño
Elevator	Ascensor/Elevador
North	Norte
South	Sur
East	Este
West	Oeste
Avenue	Avenida
Street	Calle
Boulevard	Bulevar
Cul de sac	Callejón
Cross the Street	Cruzar la calle
Pedestrians' bridge	Pasarela/puente peatonal
Traffic light	Semáforo
Far	Lejos
Close, near	Cerca
Distance	Distancia
Car	Carro/auto/coche
Bicycle	Bicicleta
Free Admission	Entrada gratis
Discount	Descuento
Children's Fare	Tarifa para niños

Chapter 4
Accommodation, Hotels and Airbnb in Latin America and Spain

The hospitality industry in Latin America and Spain is renowned for its warm and attentive service, and you can be 100% sure that you will be always treated like a special guest in ambiances that ensure your stay is both memorable and comfortable. Stepping into the realm of accommodations in Latin America and Spain, invites you to immerse yourself in diverse cultures, where understanding cultural nuances and etiquettes becomes crucial for meaningful interactions.

You will not only get a place to sleep and store your luggage, but also a support network that will make sure that you enjoy your stay. People working in the hospitality industry will be your first real contact with the local culture, and more importantly, they will also be the most willing to help you sort out every situation you might encounter. Whether you need a new towel or want to go a to hidden-gem restaurant that only locals know about, the people working in your hotel or your host in the Airbnb are the right people to ask for help.

What to expect and what to offer?

You can expect respect and courtesy, and locals will also expect to receive likewise. Respect and courtesy stand as pillars in Hispanic cultures, and embracing these values becomes paramount when engaging with hotel staff, hosts, and fellow guests. Beyond mere transactions, these cultural values lay the foundation for authentic connections and positive experiences throughout your stay. You do not want to be labeled as the person who does not say "buenos días", "buenas tardes", "buenas noches", "por favor", or "gracias". It is not that not doing this will change their attitude towards you, but being kind is a value that is expected from everyone in every interaction.

If you really want to experience this in a deeper level, we recommend you that you look for family-owned hotels. They might be smaller than other hotels, but the chance to interact with owners and workers at the same time will provide you with a unique idea of how, regardless of the position or power or wealth, everyone treats others with respect and courtesy, and how this helps to create bonds with locals in ways you cannot do it in other parts of the world.

Now, let's learn!

In this guide, we will delve into the intricacies of Spanish and Latin American hospitality, offering insights into the unique customs and expectations that shape the guest experience. By familiarizing yourself with the language of hospitality, you will not only navigate the world of accommodations with confidence but also contribute to the rich tapestry of cultural exchange.

Let's explore phrases, questions, and vocabulary tailored to the world of hotels and Airbnb stays in Latin America and Spain. By the end of this comprehensive exploration, you will possess the knowledge and language skills necessary to navigate the intricate and diverse landscape of accommodations with cultural sensitivity, ensuring that your journey is not just a physical one but also a cultural adventure that enriches your understanding of the places you visit.

Common Phrases	Translation
May I have the name for the reservation?	¿Cuál es el nombre de la reservación?
My reservation is for [Your Name].	Mi reservación es para …
I'm here to check in.	Estoy aquí para hacer el check in.
I'm here to check out.	Estoy aquí para hacer el check out.
What time is the check in?	¿A qué hora es el check in?
What time is the check out?	¿A qué hora es el check out?
Can I have an early check in?	¿Puedo hacer el check in más temprano?
Can I check out early?	¿Puedo hacer el check out más tarde?
Can I have a late check out?	¿Puedo tener un check out tardío?
Please, confirm my reservation.	Por favor, confirme mi reservación.
Can I pay with a debit card?	¿Puedo pagar con una tarjeta de débito?
Can I pay with my credit card miles?	¿Puedo pagar con una tarjeta de crédito?
Can I pay with my credit card points?	¿Puedo pagar con los puntos de mi tarjeta?
What documents do you need?	¿Qué documentos necesita?
Can I have my documents back?	¿Puede entregarme mis documentos?
Here you have my passport.	Aquí tiene mi pasaporte.
Do you have room service?	¿Tienen servicio a la habitación?
Is there room service every day?	¿Hay servicio a la habitación todos los días?
What is my room number?	¿Cuál es el número de mi habitación?
Here you have your room key.	Aquí tiene la llave de su habitación.
Can I have more than one key?	¿Me puede dar más de una llave?
What is the Wi-Fi password?	¿Cuál es la contraseña del Wi-Fi?
Is breakfast included?	¿El desayuno está incluido?
I would like to get more towels.	Me podría dar más toallas.
I need more towels.	Necesito más toallas.
How often do you change the bedding?	¿Qué tan frecuentemente se cambia la ropa de cama?
I need to change the bedding, please.	Necesito cambiar la ropa de cama, por favor.
How do I turn on the air conditioning?	¿Cómo enciendo el aire acondicionado?
How do I turn on the heating?	¿Cómo enciendo la calefacción?
How do I use the remote control for the AC?	¿Cómo uso el control remoto para el aire acondicionado?
How do I use the remote control for the TV?	¿Cómo uso el control remoto para la televisión?
The remote control needs batteries.	El control remoto necesita baterías.
Can you show me how to use the shower?	¿Puede mostrarme cómo usar la ducha?
Can I keep the windows open?	¿Puedo mantener las ventanas abiertas?

My room is too hot.	Mi habitación está demasiado caliente.
My room is too cold.	Mi habitación está demasiado fría.
How do I use the telephone in my room?	¿Cómo uso el teléfono en mi habitación?
Can I make domestic calls free of charge?	¿Puedo hacer llamadas locales gratuitas?
What is the charge for international calls?	¿Cuál es el cargo por llamadas internacionales?
What is the desk number?	¿Cuál es el número de la recepción?
Is there a kitchen?	¿Hay una cocina?
Is there a refrigerator?	¿Hay un refrigerador?
Are there hangers in the closet?	¿Hay percheros/ganchos en el armario/closet?
Is there a hairdryer?	¿Hay una secadora de cabello?
Is there a mirror?	¿Hay un espejo?
What are the breakfast hours?	¿Cuáles son las horas del desayuno?
Breakfast service is from 7 a.m. to 10 a.m.	El servicio de desayuno es de 7 am a 10 am.
Where are the restaurants nearby?	¿Dónde están los restaurantes cercanos?
What public transportation options are available to major tourist attractions nearby?	¿Qué opciones de transporte público hay para las atracciones turísticas cercanas?
How close is the bus station?	¿Qué tan cerca está la estación de buses?
How close is the metro station?	¿Qué tan cerca está la estación de metro?
How much is the bus fare?	¿Cuál es la tarifa del bus?
How do I contact you in case of emergency?	¿Cómo lo contacto en caso de emergencia?
How do I get to the [destination] from this hotel?	¿Cómo llego a [destino] desde este hotel?
Where is the nearest ATM?	¿Dónde está el cajero automático más cercano?
Can I pay with cash?	¿Puedo pagar con efectivo?
Do you accept credit cards?	¿Aceptan tarjetas de crédito?
When does the swimming pool open?	¿Cuándo abre la piscina/alberca?
When does the restaurant open?	¿Cuándo abre el restaurante?
When does the bar open?	¿Cuándo abre el bar?
When does the museum open?	¿Cuándo abre el museo?
How much is the parking fee?	¿Cuál es la tarifa del estacionamiento?
Can I park in the area?	¿Puedo estacionarme en el área?
Can I log into my streaming service accounts?	¿Puedo abrir sesión en mis cuentas de streaming?
When is room cleaning done during my stay?	¿Cuándo se hace la limpieza a la habitación durante mi estancia?
Is there a coffee machine in the room?	¿Hay una cafetera en la habitación?
Can I have food from restaurants delivered to my room through room service?	¿Puedo recibir comida de restaurantes externos a través del servicio a la habitación?
Do you have tourist brochures?	¿Tienen brochures/folletos para turistas?

What guided tour do you recommend?	¿Qué tour guiado recomiendan?
Where is the elevator?	¿Dónde está el ascensor/elevador?
Where is the emergency exit?	¿Dónde está la salida de emergencia?
I do not need more towels.	No necesito más toallas.
Can I smoke in the hotel?	¿Puedo fumar en el hotel?
Where are the designated smoking areas?	¿Dónde está la zona designada para fumadores?
I would like to add more days to my reservation.	Me gustaría agregar más días a mi reservación.
I would like to modify my reservation.	Me gustaría modificar mi reservación.
I'd like to make a dinner reservation.	Me gustaría hacer una reservación para la cena.
What are some places worth visiting in the area?	¿Qué lugares vale la pena visitar en el área?
Can you call me a taxi?	¿Puede llamar un taxi?
Do you work directly with a taxi company?	¿Trabajan directamente con una compañía de taxi?
Where is the largest shopping mall?	¿Dónde está el centro comercial más grande?
What are the room amenities?	¿Cuáles son las amenidades de la habitación?
Do you provide barbecue facilities?	¿Tienen un lugar para hacer barbacoas?
Do you have a conference room?	¿Tienen un salón de conferencias?
How reliable is the Internet?	¿Qué tan estable es el Internet?
How fast is the Internet?	¿Qué tan rápido es el Internet?
Where are the good places for a stroll nearby?	¿Cuáles son los mejores lugares para caminar?
Does this hotel/Airbnb have activities for children?	¿Este hotel/Airbnb tiene actividades para niños?
Where are the art galleries or museums nearby?	¿Dónde están las galerías o museos cercanos?
Is there a safe in the room?	¿Hay una caja fuerte en la habitación?
What type of complementary breakfast do you offer?	¿Qué tipo de desayuno complementario ofrecen?
Can I request a different breakfast if I want to?	¿Puedo pedir un desayuno diferente si lo deseo?
What is the most famous restaurant in the city?	¿Cuál es el restaurante más famoso de la ciudad?
What is the most famous museum in the city?	¿Cuál es el museo más famoso de la ciudad?
Do you offer spa services?	¿Ofrecen servicios de spa?
Do you have a sauna?	¿Tienen sauna?
What is the closest park?	¿Cuál es el parque más cercano?
What is the closest café?	¿Cuál es la cafetería más cercana?
Where is the closest Starbucks?	¿Cuál es el Starbucks más cercano?
Is the city bike-friendly?	¿Es la ciudad amigable con los ciclistas?
Where can I rent a bike?	¿Dónde puedo rentar una bicicleta?
Where can I rent a scooter?	¿Dónde puedo rentar un scooter?

Where can I rent a car?	¿Dónde puedo rentar un carro/auto/coche?
How do I get to the beach?	¿Cómo llego a la playa?
How do I get to the lake?	¿Cómo llego al lago?
Does this hotel/Airbnb provide facilities for people with disabilities?	¿Este hotel/Airbnb ofrece instalaciones para personas con discapacidad?
Does this hotel/Airbnb offer ski equipment rental services?	¿Este hotel/Airbnb ofrece servicios de renta de equipo para esquiar?
Where is the golf course nearby?	¿Dónde está el campo de golf más cercano?
Where is the souvenir shop?	¿Dónde está la tienda de recuerdos?
Do you have a souvenir shop in the hotel?	¿Tienen una tienda de recuerdos en el hotel?
What is the price range for the souvenirs in the shops?	¿Cuál es el rango de precios para los recuerdos en las tiendas?
Where can I hire an airport shuttle?	¿Dónde puedo contratar transporte para el aeropuerto?
Do you offer a shuttle service?	¿Ofrecen transporte para el aeropuerto?
Is the airport shuttle service free?	¿El trasporte para el aeropuerto es gratuito?
Where do locals go?	¿A dónde van los locales?
Where do locals eat?	¿Dónde comen los locales?
What do locals do on the weekends?	¿Qué hacen los locales los fines de semana?
What is the snowboard equipment rental fee?	¿Cuál es el precio del alquiler del equipo de snowboard?
What is the surf equipment rental fee?	¿Cuál es el precio del alquiler del equipo de surf?
What is the outdoor equipment rental fee?	¿Cuál es el precio del alquiler del equipo de senderismo?
Where are the cultural centers or art spaces nearby?	¿Cuáles son los centros o espacios culturales cercanos?
Does this hotel/Airbnb provide complementary water bottles?	¿Este hotel/Airnbnb ofrece botellas de agua complementarias?

Vocabulary	Translation
Hotel Airbnb	Hotel Airbnb
Reservation	Reservación
Check-in	Check-in
Check-out	Check-out
Room	Habitación
Room number	Número de habitación

Bed	Cama
Window	Ventana
Toilet	Baño
Shower	Ducha
Sink	Lavamanos
Towel	Toalla
Hand towel	Toalla para las manos
Bathing robe	Bata de baño
Fridge	Refrigerador
Mini fridge	Mini-refri
Kitchen	Cocina
Internet	Internet
Internet password	Clave del Internet
Breakfast	Desayuno
Breakfast included	Desayuno incluido
Breakfast time	Hora del desayuno
Room service	Servicio a la habitación
Parking	Parqueo/ Estacionamiento
Parking included	Parqueo/ Estacionamiento incluido
Parking fee	Costo del parqueo/ estacionamiento
Lobby	Recepción
Elevator	Ascensor/elevador
Smoking allowed area	Área/Zona de fumadores
Non-smoking area	Área/Zona de no fumadores
Pool	Piscina/Alberca
Gym	Gimnasio
Sauna	Sauna
Balcony	Balcón
TV	Televisión
Remote control	Control remoto
Coffee machine	Cafetera
Bottled water	Agua embotellada
Soap	Jabón
Hand soap	Jabón para manos
Shampoo	Shampoo
Conditioner	Acondicionador
Slippers	Pantuflas

Credit card	Tarjeta de crédito
Cash	Efectivo
Sofa	Sofá
Safe	Caja fuerte
Bar	Bar
Playground	Área de juegos para niños
Minibar	Minibar
Curtains	Cortinas
Noise	Ruido
Noise-cancelling Windows	Ventanas antiruido
Hairdryer	Secador de cabello
Extra towels	Toallas adicionales
Restaurant	Restaurante
Desk number	Número de recepción
24-hour service	Servicio las 24 horas

Chapter 5
Food, Restaurants, and Cafés

Food serves as the heartbeat of the Latin American and the Spaniard cultures, where the act of sharing meals with friends and family stands as a cherished tradition. Whether you're a passionate food enthusiast or someone looking to navigate the rich culinary tapestry while exploring Latin America and Spain, we are here to equip you with the language skills necessary to confidently communicate in restaurants, order your favorite dishes, and fully immerse yourself in the delightful world of Latin American and Spanish cuisine.

Throughout this chapter, we will delve into a variety of topics related to food and dining in Spain and Latin America. Here's a sneak peek at what lies ahead:

Foundations of Food Vocabulary: We will provide you with a robust foundation of Spanish and Latin American food-related vocabulary, empowering you to identify ingredients, dishes, and flavors with ease.

Mastering the Art of Ordering: Whether you find yourself in a traditional Spanish *tapas* bar, a vibrant Latin American *mercado*, or enjoying street food from a local vendor, you'll master the art of placing orders in Spanish and confidently navigating menus.

Expressing Your Preferences: Discover how to confidently convey your food preferences, allergies, and dietary restrictions, ensuring that each meal caters to your tastes and requirements.

Asking Informed Questions: Equip yourself with the ability to ask questions about the menu, ingredients, and preparation methods, enabling you to make informed choices and engage in meaningful conversations with local chefs and fellow diners.

By the time you reach the end of this chapter, you'll be well-prepared to savor the diverse and delectable dishes that Spain and Latin America have to offer. You'll not only navigate the world of food and dining with ease but also engage in meaningful conversations with locals, forging connections through the universal language of cuisine. Together, we will build your conversational skills and explore the tantalizing world of Spanish and Latin American food! ¡Buen *provecho!*

Common Phrases	Translation
Can I have the menu, please?	¿Me puede dar un menú, por favor?
Do you have free tables?	¿Tiene mesas libres?
Do you have tables by the windows/balcony?	¿Tiene mesas cerca de la ventana/del balcón?
I am ready to order.	Estoy listo para ordenar.
I'd like to order.	Me gustaría ordenar.
Can we I have two more minutes? I'm not ready to order yet.	¿Me puede dar dos minutos más? Todavía no estoy listo para ordenar.
What is the most popular dish?	¿Cuál es el plato más popular?
What do you recommend?	¿Qué es lo que recomienda?
What is this?	¿Qué es esto?

Is this spicy?	¿Es picante?
Can you make it spicier?	¿Puede hacerlo más picante?
Can you make it less spicy?	¿Puede hacerlo menos picante?
I'll take this to go.	Quiero esto para llevar.
Can I have a box/bag for this?	¿Me puede dar una bolsa/caja para esto?
Can I have the bill, please?	¿Me puede traer la cuenta, por favor?
I'm ready to pay.	Estoy listo para pagar.
I'd like to pay.	Me gustaría pagar.
Do you accept credit cards?	¿Aceptan tarjetas de crédito?
Should I pay here at the table or at the cashier?	¿Debo pagar aquí o en el cajero?
We only accept cash.	Sólo aceptamos efectivo.
Tips are included in the bill.	La propina está incluida en la cuenta.
Tips are voluntary.	Las propinas son voluntarias.
The food here is good.	Aquí la comida es buena.
The meal was delicious.	La comida estuvo deliciosa.
I'm vegetarian.	Soy vegetariano(a).
I'm vegan.	Soy vegano(a).
I don't eat meat.	No como carne.
I have allergies to…	Tengo alergia a la…
I'd like to drink…	Me gustaría beber …
I would like to have some water.	Me gustaría un poco de agua.
I'd like a cup of wine…	Me gustaría una copa de vino.
To drink, I want a carbonated water.	Para beber, quiero agua carbonatada/mineral.
Can I have cold water?	¿Puede darme agua helada?
One bottle of water, please.	Una botella de agua, por favor.
It smells good.	Huele bien.
Please, I need some extra sauce.	Por favor, necesito salsa extra.
Can you pass me the salt?	¿Puede pasarme la sal?
Can you pass me the pepper?	¿Puede pasarme la pimienta?
What is the most popular dish?	¿Cuál es el plato más popular?
I'd like to have a coffee.	Me gustaría un café.
I'd like to have an expresso.	Me gustaría un expresso.
I'd like to have an Americano.	Me gustaría un café americano.
How much is this?	¿Cuánto cuesta esto?
What time do you close?	¿A qué hora cierran?
What time do you open?	¿A qué hora abren?
I want to order some dessert.	Quiero algo de postre.

Can I have an extra spoon?	¿Me puede dar una cuchara extra?
Can I have an extra fork?	¿Me puede dar un tenedor extra?
Can I have an extra plate?	¿Me puede dar un plato extra?
Can I have more napkins?	¿Me puede dar más servilletas?
I'm sorry.	Lo siento.
Thank you so much!	¡Muchas gracias!
Can you repeat that, please?	¿Puede repetir eso, por favor?
The food is to go.	La comida es para llevar.
I would like to make a reservation.	Me gustaría hacer una reservación.
Please, pack this to go.	Por favor, empaque esto para llevar.
Do you need anything else?	¿Necesita algo más?
Would you like to order anything else?	¿Le gustaría ordenar algo más?
When will the food be ready?	¿Cuándo estará lista la comida?
You will have to wait a little longer than usual.	Tendrá que esperar un poco más de lo habitual.
How is this dish prepared?	¿Cómo se prepara este platillo?
Does it contain…?	¿Contiene …?
White rice, please!	Arroz blanco, ¡por favor!
I want scrambled eggs.	Quiero huevos revueltos.
I want scrambled eggs with ham.	Quiero huevos revueltos con jamón.
I want sunny-side eggs.	Quiero huevos estrellados.
It is my first time trying this kind of food.	Es mi primera vez probando este tipo de comida.
I'm loving it!	¡Me gusta!
What types of bread do you have?	¿Qué tipo de pan tiene?
Does it contain caffeine?	¿Contiene cafeína?
I would like to try some street food.	Me gustaría probar la comida callejera.
Where can I order pizza?	¿Dónde puedo ordenar pizza?
What are the healthy options?	¿Cuáles son las opciones saludables?
I'd like to order a sweet dessert.	Me gustaría ordenar un postre dulce.
I can't eat dairy products.	No puedo comer productos lácteos.
Can I have a salad, please?	¿Me puede dar una ensalada, por favor?
Do you have a kids' menu?	¿Tiene un menú para niños?
Please, add more cheese.	Por favor, agregue más queso.
Do you have a buffet?	¿Tiene un bufet?
Are the drinks unlimited?	¿Las bebidas son ilimitadas?
I would like to add something to my order…	Me gustaría agregar algo a mi orden…
Where is the bathroom?	¿Dónde está el baño?

Where can I pay?	¿Dónde puedo pagar?
The place is beautiful.	Este lugar es bonito.
I'll leave a positive review!	Dejaré una reseña positiva.
I'd definitively come back!	¡Definitivamente, volvería de nuevo!
I'd love the service!	¡Me encantó el servicio!

Common Vocabulary	Translation
Food	Comida
Breakfast	Desayuno
Lunch	Almuerzo
Dinner	Cena
Snack	Bocadillo
Meat	Carne
Chicken	Pollo
Beef	Carne de res
Pork	Carne de cerdo
Fish	Pescado
Vegetables	Vegetales
Onion	Cebolla
Carrot	Zanahoria
Mushroom	Hongos
Pepper	Chiles
Jalapeno	Jalapeño
Lettuce	Lechuga
Cabbage	Repollo
Tomato	Tomate
Tomato sauce	Salsa de tomate
Milk	Leche
Cheese	Queso
Cream	Crema
Butter	Mantequilla
Egg	Huevo
Bread	Pan
Fruit	Fruta
Apple	Manzana
Banana	Banana
Pear	Pera

Watermelon	Sandía
Melon	Melón
Pineapple	Piña
Strawberry	Fresa
Beans	Frijoles
Rice	Arroz
Pasta	Pasta
Salt	Sal
Pepper	Pimienta
Sugar	Azúcar
Oil	Aceite
Vinegar	Vinagre
Garlic	Ajo
Spices	Especias
Seasoning	Sasonador
Dressing	Aderezo
Salad	Ensalada
Menu	Menú
Restaurant	Restaurante
Café	Cafetería
Bakery	Panadería
Butchery	Carnicería
Soup	Sopa
Appetizer	Aperitivo/entrada
Main Dish	Plato principal
Dessert	Postre
Wine	Vino
Water	Agua
Carbonated water	Agua carbonatada/mineral
Cider	Sidra
Grilled	Asado, a la parrilla
Baked	Horneado
Steamed	Al vapor
Well-done	Bien cocido
Half-done	Término medio
Stew	Estofado, guisado
Sushi	Sushi

Sandwich	Emparedado, sándwich
Ham	Jamón
Toast	Tostada, pan tostado
Spoon	Cuchara
Fork	Tenedor
Knife	Cuchillo
Plate	Plato
Cup	Taza
Napkin	Servilleta
Glass	Vaso
Cutlery	Cubiertos
Kitchen	Cocina
Ice cream	Helado
Cake	Pastel/torta
Hamburger	Hamburguesa
Typical food	Comida típica
Street food	Comida callejera
Bacon	Tocino

Chapter 6
The Shopping Experience in Spanish-Speaking Countries

In both Spain and Latin America, shopping transcends the act of mere transactions; it's a cultural odyssey waiting to be explored. Trust us, you have never experienced shopping as you will in a Spanish-speaking country. You will love it and will want to go back to it as soon as you can. Whether you're a fashion enthusiast tracking the latest trends or a collector in search of unique treasures, there's an adventure tailored to everyone's tastes.

From navigating the bustling traditional markets of Mexico City, San Jose, Bogota, or Lima, to exploring the charming boutiques of Barcelona, Buenos Aires, or Guatemala, or wandering through the modern shopping malls of San Salvador or Santiago de Chile, this chapter aims to empower you to interact confidently with locals and shopkeepers alike. With a diverse array of shopping experiences, spanning the historic markets of Seville to the vibrant artisan markets of Oaxaca, you'll learn the nuances of greeting and engaging with shopkeepers and fellow shoppers.

Discover how to inquire about product details, sizes, and prices, adeptly negotiate and bargain, express your preferences with cultural finesse, make informed purchasing decisions, seek guidance in sprawling shopping centers, and grasp the essential vocabulary for various shopping scenarios.

Whether you're on the hunt for the latest fashion trends, traditional crafts from Spain or Latin America, or simply looking to immerse yourself in the dynamic market cultures, our guide is designed to empower you to make the most of your shopping experiences across the Spanish-speaking regions, combining the rich tapestry of Spain and the diverse flavors of Latin America.

Common Phrases	Translation
How much is it?	¿Cuánto cuesta?
How much is it?	¿Cuánto vale?
What is the price?	¿Cuál es el precio?
Does it have a discount?	¿Tiene descuento?
Can you give me a discount?	¿Puede darme un descuento?
Do you have this in a different color?	¿Tiene esto en un color diferente?
Do you have this in a different size?	¿Tiene esto en un tamaño diferente?
Can I pay with cash?	¿Puedo pagar con efectivo?
Can I pay with credit card?	¿Puedo pagar con tarjeta de crédito?
Can I pay with my credit card point?	¿Puedo pagar con los puntos de mi tarjeta de crédito?
Can I pay with my credit card miles?	¿Puedo pagar con las millas de mi tarjeta de crédito?
Do you offer loyalty reward points?	¿Ofrecen puntos de recompensa por fidelidad?
Here you have your receipt.	Aquí está su recibo.
Here you have your product.	Aquí está su producto.
Do you need a bag?	¿Necesita una bolsa?
Is this the final price?	¿Este es el precio final?

Does the price include taxes?	¿El precio incluye impuestos?
The price does not include taxes.	El precio no incluye impuestos.
Is there a discount for bulk purchases?	¿Hay un descuento por comprar a mayor?
I need a receipt, please.	Necesito la factura, por favor.
Can I try it?	¿Puedo probarlo?
Can I try in on?	¿Puedo probármelo?
Where is the fitting room?	¿Dónde está el probador?
Do you have this in a bigger size?	¿Tiene esto en un tamaño más grande?
Do you have this in a smaller size?	¿Tiene esto en un tamaño más pequeño?
Do you accept returns?	¿Aceptan devoluciones?
What is the return policy?	¿Cuál es la política de devolución?
We do not accept returns.	No aceptamos devoluciones.
We accept returns if the product still has the tags.	Aceptamos devoluciones si el producto aún tiene las etiquetas.
How long is the sale going on?	¿Cuánto tiempo estará la promoción?
How long will the discount last?	¿Cuánto tiempo estará el descuento?
What is the most popular brand?	¿Cuál es la marca más popular?
What is the most popular product?	¿Cuál es el producto más popular?
What material is it made of?	¿De qué material está hecho?
It is made of synthetic material.	Está hecho con material sintético.
It is made of leather.	Está hecho con cuero.
It is made of denim.	Está hecho con mezclilla.
I like this handbag.	Me gusta esta bolsa.
I like those shoes.	Me gustan esos zapatos.
I don't like the wallet.	No me gusta la billetera/cartera.
I don't like these pants.	No me gustan estos pantalones.
Does the product have warranty?	¿El producto tiene garantía?
How long does the warranty last?	¿Cuánto dura la garantía?
Can I see it?	¿Puedo verlo?
Can you show that product over there?	¿Puede mostrarme ese producto de allá?
You can see it.	Puede verlo.
You can try it.	Puede probarlo.
It is not for sale.	No está a la venta.
Is it for sale?	¿Está a la venta?
What is the lowest price?	¿Cuál es el precio más bajo?
What is the best price you can offer?	¿Cuál es el mejor precio que puede ofrecer?

Can I find this product in other stores?	¿Puedo encontrar este producto en otras tiendas?
It is an exclusive product.	Es un producto exclusivo.
It is not available in other stores.	No está disponible en otras tiendas.
This is a perfect gift.	Este es un regalo perfecto.
It is a unique gift.	Es un regalo único.
What do you recommend?	¿Qué me recomienda?
What time does the shop open?	¿A qué hora abre la tienda?
What time does the shop close?	¿A qué hora cierra la tienda?
Is it open during the weekends?	¿Está abierto los fines de semana?
This is the best price.	Este es el mejor precio.
It is a reasonable price.	Es un precio razonable.
You will not find a better price.	No va a encontrar un precio mejor.
It is really beautiful.	Es muy bonito.
It is really special.	Es muy especial.
It represents our culture.	Representa nuestra cultura.
It is a traditional dress.	Es un vestido tradicional.
It is a traditional hat.	Es un sombrero tradicional.
Can you ship it to my country?	¿Puede enviarlo a mi país?
How much is the shipping to my country?	¿Cuánto cuesta el envío a mi país?
What is the weight of this?	¿Cuánto pesa este producto?
Where is this made?	¿Dónde se fabrica?
How do I have to take care of it?	¿Cómo debo cuidarlo?
Can I see it first?	¿Puedo verlo primero?
Can I open the package?	¿Puedo abrir el empaque?
You cannot open the package, but I have a product sample.	No puede abrir el empaque, pero tengo un producto de muestra.
What type of sounds does it make?	¿Qué tipo de sonido hace?
Does it have special features?	¿Tiene características especiales?
Is this a new product?	¿Este producto es nuevo?
Can you wrap it as a present?	¿Puede envolverlo para regalo?
Does it have an additional cost?	¿Tiene un costo adicional?
I can wrap it as a present with no additional cost.	Puedo envolverlo para regalo sin costo adicional.
Do you accept discount coupons?	¿Aceptan cupones de descuento?
Can I have a better price if I buy more than one?	¿Me puede dar un mejor precio si compro más de uno?
How long does the shipping take?	¿Cuánto tarda la entrega?

Is it available online?	¿Está disponible en línea?
Is it sold on the Internet?	¿Se vende por Internet?
Is it safe for kids?	¿Es seguro para los niños?
The product is for 3-year-old kids or older.	El producto es para niños mayores de 3 años.
The product is not safe for kids.	El producto no es seguro para niños.
It is not a safe product for carry-on luggage.	No es un producto seguro para el equipaje de mano.
Is there any type of allergic reaction?	¿Hay algún tipo de reacción alérgica?
What type of warranty does the product have?	¿Qué tipo garantía tiene el producto?
What type of warranty do you offer?	¿Qué tipo de garantía ofrece usted?
Can it be customized?	¿Se puede personalizar?
Can my name be engraved?	¿Se puede grabar mi nombre?
What is the return policy?	¿Cuál es la política de devolución?
Can I pay with dollars?	¿Puedo pagar con dólares?
Can I pay with the local currency?	¿Puedo pagar con la moneda local?
Are taxes included?	¿Los impuestos están incluidos?
Is this the final price?	¿Es este el precio final?
The best store in the city is…	La mejor tienda de la ciudad es…
The best shopping mall in the city is…	El mejor centro comercial de la ciudad es…
How do you use it?	¿Cómo se usa?
How do you eat it?	¿Cómo se come?
The telephone price is…	El precio del teléfono es…
The book price is…	El precio del libro es…
It has special features.	Tiene características especiales.
It is a traditional product.	Es un producto tradicional.
This is the best store in the country.	Esta es la mejor tienda del país.
This is the most exclusive product we have.	Es el producto más exclusivo que tenemos.
Add it to my bill.	Agréguelo a mi cuenta.
I won't buy it.	No lo compraré.
I don't need it.	No lo necesito.
I'll pick it up tomorrow.	Lo recogeré mañana.

Common Vocabulary	Translation
Shopping	Compras
Store	Tienda
Shopping mall	Centro comercial
Market	Mercado

Open-air market	Mercado al aire libre
Supermarket	Supermercado
Product	Producto
Price	Precio
Package	Empaque
Box	Caja
Tag	Etiqueta
Sell	Venta
Transaction	Transacción
Payment	Pago
Pay with cash	Pago en efectivo
Pay with card	Pago con tarjeta
Receipt	Recibo
Reimbursement	Reembolso
Warranty	Garantía
Size	Tamaño
Color	Color
Shape	Forma
Brand	Marca
Style	Estilo
Origin	Origen
Model	Modelo
Manufacturing date	Fecha de fabricación
Manufacturing place	Lugar de fabricación
Expiration date	Fecha de expiración
To try something on	Probarse algo
Features	Características
Special features	Características especiales
Material	Material
Fabric	Tela
Denim	Mezclilla
Polyester	Poliéster
Synthetic	Sintético
Leather	Cuero
Wool	Lana
Seller	Vendedor
Consumer	Consumidor

Event	Evento
Coupon	Cupón
Discount coupon	Cupón de descuento
Deposit	Depósito
Installment	Cuota
Interest-free installment	Cuotas/Meses sin intereses
Exchange	Intercambio
Quality	Calidad
Quantity	Cantidad
Variety	Variedad
Unbox	Desempacar
Exchange rate	Tasa/Tipo de cambio
Local currency	Moneda local
Dollars	Dólares
Euros	Euros
Wholesale discount	Descuento por mayoreo
Unit discount	Descuento por unidad
Shop owner	Propietario
Credit card points	Puntos de trarjeta de crédito
Credit card miles	Millas de tarjeta de crédito
Loyalty points	Puntos de lealtad
Return	Devolución
Return policy	Política de devolución
Defect	Defecto
Sleeve	Manga
Long sleeve	Manga larga
Short sleeve	Manga corta
Sleeveless	Sin manga
Shopping kart	Carro de compras
ATM	Cajero automático
Watch	Reloj
Wristwatch	Reloj de pulsera
Bracelet	Brazalete
Shoe	Zapato
Sole	Suela
Shoelace	Cinta de zapato, agujeta
High heel	Zapato de tacón

Sandal / Flip flops	Sandalia
Ring	Anillo
Earrings	Aretes
Hat	Sombrero
Beach hat	Sombrero de playa
Bag	Bolsa
Scarf	Bufanda
Sweater	Suéter
Coat	Abrigo
Wallet	Billetera, cartera (Mexico)
Purse	Cartera (Spain), bolsa
Shirt	Camisa
T-shirt	Camiseta, playera
Skirt	Falda
Dress	Vestido
Pants	Pantalones
Suit	Traje
Belt	Cinturón
Formal shoes	Zapatos formales
Sneakers	Zapatos deportivos, tenis
Swimsuit	Traje de baño, bañador
Lingerie	Lencería
Underwear	Ropa interior
Baseball cap	Gorra
Headphones	Audífonos
Speaker	Bocina
Phone	Teléfono
Computer	Computadora
Laptop	Computadora portátil
Book	Libro
Bestseller book	Libro más vendido
Inventory	Inventario
Customer satisfaction	Satisfacción del cliente
Review	Reseña
Product review	Reseña del producto
Store review	Reseña de la tienda
Order number	Número de orden

Date of delivery	Fecha de entrega
Receipt verification	Verificación del recibo
Cashier	Caja registradora
Free sale	Venta libre
Value for money	Valor por dinero
Seasonal sale	Venta de temporada
Brand logo	Logo de la marca
Price comparison	Comparación de precio
Fitting room	Probador
Manager	Gerente
Sale advisor	Asesor de compras
Consumer protection	Protección al consumidor
Price adjustment	Ajuste de precio
Free trial	Prueba gratis
Offer	Promoción
On sale	Liquidación
Advertisement	Anuncio
Reward program	Programa de recompensas
Order confirmation	Confirmación del pedido
Withdrawal	Retiro
Money withdrawal	Retiro de dinero
Window-shop	Ir de tienda en tienda

Chapter 7
Drugstores and Hospital Visits in Spanish-Speaking Countries

Latin America and Spain are renowned for their rich history, vibrant cuisine, and breathtaking landscapes, there is also a thriving drinking culture that plays a significant role in the social fabric of the nation. People in these regions are known for their strong sense of community and the tendency to form connections over shared meals or rounds of drinks. Whether it's enjoying a bottle of wine, savoring local beer, or indulging in beloved traditional dishes, these communal gatherings provide opportunities for connection, celebration, and relaxation from the demands of daily life. However, a night of merriment can sometimes lead to the famous "Spanish hangover," an experience that can be challenging for visitors who are not aware of the various remedies and cures available.

Other emergencies are possible as well. Navigating a hospital or pharmacy in a foreign country can be a daunting task, especially when you're not feeling well. With these questions and phrases, you will gain the confidence to express your needs, symptoms, and concerns effectively in Spanish, ensuring a positive experience during medical visits.

We want to emphasize this: we hope you never need these phrases for yourself, and that your trip to any Spanish-speaking country is full of wonderful experiences. However, we are aware that sometimes not everything goes as planned – you might get sick, have an accident, get food-poisoned, or even drink more than you intended too. If something like happens, we got you covered with all the phrases and vocabulary that you will learn in this chapter.

Common Phrases	Translation
I need help.	Necesito ayuda.
I need medical help.	Necesito ayuda médica.
I need to see a doctor.	Necesito ver a un doctor.
I need to go to a hospital.	Necesito ir a un hospital.
Please, call a doctor.	Por favor, llame a un doctor.
Please, take me to an emergency room.	Por favor, lléveme a una sala de emergencia.
I have so much pain.	Tengo mucho dolor.
I have fever.	Tengo fiebre.
I have a headache.	Me duele la cabeza.
I have a back pain.	Me duele la espalda.
My feet hurt.	Me duelen los pies.
I have a stomachache.	Me duele el estómago.
My belly hurts.	Me duele el vientre.
I have cramps.	Tengo calambres.
I broke my arm.	Me fracturé un brazo.
I broke my shoulder.	Me fracturé un hombro.
I broke my leg.	Me fracturé una pierna.
I need to vomit.	Necesito vomitar.

I have nauseas.	Tengo náuseas.
I feel dizzy.	Me siendo mareado.
I am going to throw up.	Voy a vomitar.
I have diarrhea.	Tengo diarrea.
I am dehydrated.	Estoy deshidratado(a).
I have a running nose.	Tengo la nariz congestionada.
I have an allergy.	Tengo una alergia.
I have a cold.	Tengo un resfriado.
I'm in too much pain to move.	No puedo moverme por el dolor.
I have diabetes.	Tengo diabetes.
My sugar level is high.	Tengo la azúcar alta.
My sugar level is low.	Tengo la azúcar baja.
My blood pressure is high.	Tengo la presión alta.
My blood pressure is low.	Tengo la presión baja.
I feel weak.	Me siento débil.
I am sick.	Estoy enfermo(a).
I am bleeding.	Estoy sangrando.
I need a thermometer.	Necesito un termómetro.
Can you give me a prescription?	¿Puede darme una prescripción/receta?
I need medication for…	Necesito medicina para…
What is the recommended dose?	¿Cuál es la dosis recomendada?
You need to take this pill after eating.	Necesita tomar la pastilla después de comer.
You need to take this pill before eating.	Necesita tomar la pastilla antes de comer.
You need to take this test before having breakfast.	Necesita hacerse el examen/estudio antes del desayuno.
You need to take this test after having breakfast.	Necesita hacerse el examen/estudio después del desayuno.
I am allergic to…	Soy alérgico a…
I have allergies to…	Tengo alergias a…
I need a pill to sleep.	Necesito una pastilla para dormir.
Where can I buy this medication?	¿Dónde puedo comprar este medicamento?
I have a horrible hangover.	Tengo una resaca/cruda horrible.
I need to drink electrolytes.	Necesito beber electrolitos.
I need a glass of water.	Necesito un vaso de agua.
I need dan energy drink.	Necesito una bebida energizante.
The patient needs to rest.	El paciente necesita descansar.
You need to rest.	Usted necesita descansar.

I need to sleep.	Necesito dormir.
I feel weak. I need to sit.	Me siento débil. Necesito sentarme.
What is the treatment?	¿Cuál es el tratamiento?
What is the treatment price?	¿Cuál es el precio del tratamiento?
How long should I take the treatment?	¿Cuántos días necesito tomar el tratamiento?
What is the recovery period?	¿Cuál es el periodo de recuperación?
The recovery is fast.	La recuperación es rápida.
The recovery is generally slow.	La recuperación generalmente es lenta.
Do I need to register as a patient?	¿Necesito registrarme como paciente?
Where is the hospital?	¿Dónde está el hospital?
Where is the clinic?	¿Dónde está la clínica?
Where is the drugstore?	¿Dónde está la farmacia?
You need to wait for the doctor.	Usted necesita esperar al doctor.
The nurse Will take your information.	La enfermera tomará su información.
I need to be hospitalized.	Necesito ser hospitalizado.
This is my information.	Ésta es mi información.
These are my documents.	Estos son mis documentos.
The information of my medical insurance is here.	La información de mi seguro médico está aquí.
I don't have a medical insurance.	No tengo seguro médico.
I have a medical insurance.	Tengo un seguro médico.
I need a blood test,	Necesito un examen/estudio de sangre.
Can I buy this medication without a prescription?	¿Puedo comprar este medicamento sin prescripción/receta?
You can't do exercise for a month.	No puede hacer ejercicio por un mes.
You can't eat greasy food for a month.	No puede comer comida grasosa por un mes.
You can't consume alcoholic drinks for a month.	No puede consumir alcohol por un mes.
You can't make any physical effort for a month.	No puede hacer esfuerzo físico por un mes.
I need to go to a dentist.	Necesito ir a un dentista.
It is uncomfortable.	Es incómodo.
It is a severe pain.	Es un dolor grave.
I am not sick. I have a hangover.	No estoy enfermo. Tengo resaca./Estoy crudo.
Where can I see my medical records?	¿Dónde puedo ver mi historial médico?
When Will I get the results?	¿Cuándo tendré los resultados?
What is the diagnosis?	¿Cuál es el diagnóstico?
I have itching.	Tengo comezón.
Where can I buy a thermometer?	¿Dónde puedo comprar un termómetro?

Where can I buy an oximeter?	¿Dónde puedo comprar un oxímetro?
I can't breathe.	No puedo respirar.
Please, call an ambulance.	Por favor, llame a una ambulancia.
How do you feel?	¿Cómo se siente?
I feel…	Me siento…
How did the accident happen?	¿Cómo ocurrió el accidente?
Where did the accident happen?	¿Dónde ocurrió el accidente?
What happened after?	¿Qué pasó después?
Does your head hurt?	¿Le duele la cabeza?
Does your body hurt?	¿Le duele el cuerpo?
Do you have or have you had fever?	¿Tiene o ha tenido fiebre?
Can you give me an ID card?	¿Puede darme una identificación?
I feel down the stairs.	Me caí de las escaleras.
I sprained my ankle.	Me torcí un tobillo.
I need a wheelchair.	Necesito una silla de ruedas.
I think I broke my arm.	Creo que me fracturé un brazo.
I broke my leg.	Me fracturé una pierna.
I have symptoms of food poisoning.	Tengo síntomas de una intoxicación alimenticia.
My eyes are red.	Mis ojos están rojos.
I have a throat infection.	Tengo una infección en la garganta.
I have a urinary tract infection.	Tengo una infección en las vías urinarias.
The remedy is not working.	El remedio no está funcionando.
You need a surgery.	Usted necesita una cirugía.
You need to go back to your country.	Usted necesita regresar a su país.
When is your return flight?	¿Cuándo es su vuelo de regreso?
In this condition, you can't fly.	En esta condición, usted no puede volar.
What is your emergency contact information?	¿Cuál es la información de sus contactos de emergencia?
Don't worry!	¡No se preocupe!
Everything will be alright.	Todo estará bien.

Common Vocabulary	Translation
Doctor	Doctor
Nurse	Enfermera
Hospital	Hospital
Clinic	Clínica
Emergency	Emergencia

Emergency room	Sala de emergencia
Patient	Paciente
Ambulance	Ambulancia
Medical test	Examen/Estudio médico
Test	Examen/Estudio
Medication	Medicina
Pill	Pastilla
Syrup	Jarabe
Injection	Inyección
Vaccine	Vacuna
Consultation	Consulta
Hospital room	Habitación de hospital
Drugstore	Farmacia
Diagnosis	Diagnóstico
Painkiller	Analgésico
Rash	Comezón
Sleeping pill	Pastilla para dormir
Thermometer	Termómetro
Blood pressure	Presión arterial
Blood pressure monitor	Monitor de presión arterial
Vitamin	Vitamina
Type	Tipo
Dose	Dosis
Side effects	Efectos secundarios
How to take it	Cómo tomarla
After eating	Después de comer
Before eating	Antes de comer
After the shower	Después de la ducha
Before the shower	Antes de la ducha
Expiration date	Fecha de expiración
Warning	Advertencia
Oximeter	Oxímetro
Storage instructions	Instrucciones de almacenamiento
Hangover	Resaca/Cruda
Hangover remedy	Remedio para la resaca/cruda
Water	Agua
Dehydration	Deshidratación

Dehydrated	Deshidratado(a)
Pain	Dolor
Headache	Dolor de cabeza
Body ache	Dolor de cuerpo
Pain in the back	Dolor de espalda
Pain in the neck	Dolor de cuello
Stomachache	Dolor de estómago
Bellyache	Dolor de vientre
Pain in the feet	Dolor en los pies
Pain in the hands	Dolor en las manos
Food poisoning	Intoxicación alimenticia
Vomit	Vómito
Diarrhea	Diarrea
Intoxication/poisoning	Intoxicación/ Envenenamiento
Treatment	Tratamiento
To be in pain	Tener dolor
Recovery	Recuperación
X-rays	Radiografía
Tomography	Tomografía
Medical record	Historial médico
Anesthesia	Anestesia
Surgery	Cirugía
Surgeon	Cirujano
Medical insurance	Seguro médico
Insurance bill	Factura del seguro
Medical staff	Personal médico
Medical assessment	Evaluación médica
Fracture	Fractura
Broken arm	Fractura de brazo
Broken leg	Fractura de pierna
Wheelchair	Silla de ruedas
Burn	Quemadura
Wound	Herida
Accident	Accidente
Traffic accident	Accidente de tráfico
Fall	Caída
Reaction	Reacción

Allergic reaction	Reacción alérgica
Treatment reaction	Reacción al tratamiento
General doctor	Doctor general
Obstetrician/ Gynecologist	Obstetra/Ginecólogo
Dentist	Dentista
Blood type	Tipo de sangre
Infection	Infección
Effect	Efecto
Medicinal effect	Efecto medicinal
COVID test	Prueba de COVID
Pregnancy test	Prueba de embarazo
STD	ETS
Liquid	Líquido
Doctor prescription	Prescripción del doctor
Syringe	Jeringa
Diet	Dieta
Supplementary diet	Dieta suplementaria
Electrolytes	Electrolitos
Adverse reaction	Reacción adversa
Medication abuse	Abuso del medicamento
Alcohol addiction	Adicción al alcohol
Symptoms	Síntomas
Hangover symptoms	Síntomas de la resaca/cruda
Symptoms of intoxication	Síntomas de intoxicación/ envenenamiento
Symptoms of food poisoning	Síntomas de una intoxicación alimenticia
Detox drink	Bebida desintoxicante
Dizziness	Mareos
Nauseas	Náuseas
Prevention	Prevención
Gloves	Guantes
Vomit bag	Bolsa para vomitar
Remedy	Remedio
Alcohol	Alcohol
Shoulder	Hombro
Ankle	Tobillo
Eyes	Ojos
Sleep	Dormir

Treatment plan	Plan de tratamiento
Hospital bill	Factura del hospital
Covered by the insurance	Cubierto por el seguro
Blood	Sangre
Blood tests	Exámenes/estudios de sangre
Patient information	Información del paciente
See a doctor	Ver a un doctor
Consult with a doctor	Consultar con un doctor

Conclusion

In conclusion, we are pretty sure that this conversational Spanish book has been a journey of language discovery and cultural exploration. As we've navigated through various dialogues and situations you surely will encounter during your trips, you have not only honed your Spanish conversational skills but also gained a deeper understanding of the rich tapestry of Hispanic culture.

From casual chit-chat to more profound discussions, this book has equipped you with a diverse range of conversational scenarios, and we can be sure that you are ready to engage in real-life Spanish conversations. The emphasis on practical vocabulary and expressions that you have learned empowers you to communicate effectively in various social, travel, and professional situations.

Furthermore, the incorporation of cultural nuances and idiomatic expressions has not only enriched your language proficiency but has also fostered a genuine appreciation for the diverse Spanish-speaking world. Beyond just words and grammar, you've delved into the essence of communication, learning not only how to speak Spanish but also how to connect with others on a deeper level.

As we bid farewell to this conversational journey, let's carry forward the confidence gained from these dialogues into your real-life interactions. May the conversations continue to flow, bridging linguistic and cultural gaps, and may the spirit of learning and curiosity propel us to further explore the captivating world of Spanish language and culture. ¡Hasta la próxima conversación!

Spanish Short Stories For

Language Learners

Learn and Improve Your Spanish Comprehension and Vocabulary Through 30 Short Stories Based Off Captivating Spanish History

Worldwide Nomad

Introduction

present to you a mesmerising travel through the pages of stories that juxtapose the rich history of Spain with spellbinding fiction. In this book, you will find tales that not only create engaging plots, but also immerse the reader in the deep culture and identity of Spain, where the past and the imagination are mixed in a unique way. Each story not only celebrates the diversity of Spanish culture, but also highlights the importance of history as a fundamental foundation of its identity. As you delve into the pages of this book, I hope you find an understanding of Spanish culture that helps you bridge the gap between past and fiction and that makes your learning experience beautiful and rewarding.

MARA LA GRANDE

Antaño, Mara era una de las tartesias más populares jamás conocidas. No sólo era popular por su belleza, sino también por su forma de hablar y su habilidad para extraer metales. Era una época en la que los tartesios eran conocidos por cómo extraían metales y los convertían en cosas bellas. Aunque eran populares por esto, las mujeres normalmente se quedaban en casa cuidando a los niños. Pero Mara era diferente. Mara era inquieta y nunca estaba en casa. Seguía a su marido al trabajo todos los días y pronto se convirtió en una de las trabajadoras más importantes. Sus habilidades eran tan buenas que el rey Tartessos la invitó a su palacio.

Al llegar a casa, Mara le contó a su marido la invitación y decidieron ir con sus dos hijos a la capital para reunirse con el rey. Emocionado, su marido le aconsejó que vendieran su casa con la esperanza de que el rey les diera una nueva en la capital, gracias a la abundancia de sus riquezas. Así pues, fueron al mercado y vendieron todo lo que poseían, tras lo cual regalaron su casa a los pobres.

Al llegar a palacio, tal y como habían predicho, el rey les dio una nueva casa y nombró a Mara jefa del departamento de metales.

MARA THE GREAT

Once, Mara was one of the most popular Tartessians ever known. She was not only popular for her beauty, but she was also popular for her manner of speaking and her metal extraction skills. Now, this was a time when the Tartessians were known for how they extracted metal and made them into beautiful things. Although they were popular for this, the women would usually stay home and tend to the children. But Mara was different. Mara was restless and never home, she followed her husband to work every day and soon, she became one of the most important workers around. Her skills were so good that one, Tartessos the king, invited her to his palace.

On getting home, Mara told her husband of the invite and they decided to go with their two children to the capital to meet with the king. Out of excitement, her husband advised her that they should sell their home in the hope that the king would give them a new home in the capital, out of the abundance of his wealth. So, they went into the market and sold everything they owned, after which they gave their house to the poor.

On getting to the palace, just like they predicted, the king gave them a new home and appointed Mara as the head of the metals department.

Vocabulary

Popular	Popular
Vender	Sell
Palacio	Palace
Predicho	Predicted
Riqueza	Wealth
Importante	Important
Cuidar	Tend
Casa	House
Manera	Manner
Metales	Metals
Belleza	Beautiful
Pobre	Poor
Hermoso	Beautiful
Extracción	Extraction
Trabajador	Worker
Invitada	Invited

Comprehension Questions

¿Por qué eran conocidos los tartesios? What were the Tartessians known for?

¿En qué se diferenciaba Mara de los demás? How was Mara different from other people?

¿Qué hicieron Mara y su marido con su casa? What did Mara and her husband do with their home?

Historical Note

The cultures that first occupied the Iberain peninsula were the Iberians, the celts, the Lusitanians and the Tartessians. The Tartessians, centred around the Guadalquivir River, were known for advanced metallurgy, and they engaged in extensive trade around 1000 BCE.

AMISTADES Y AMOR

Cartago era una de las pequeñas ciudades del norte de África hace mucho tiempo, y en ella vivían Juan y su amigo Luis. Ambos eran amigos desde la infancia, ya que nacieron con pocos días de diferencia y crecieron juntos como vecinos. Todo el mundo los conocía y, con el tiempo, empezaron a parecerse tanto que la gente los llamaba gemelos. Ahora, ambos habían crecido y se habían convertido en uno de los comerciantes cartagineses, en una época en la que Carthago Nova se convirtió en un importante centro comercial que conectaba la Península Ibérica con la amplia red comercial cartaginesa.

Mientras Juan comerciaba con joyas, Luis lo hacía con sales y, juntos, se convirtieron en ricos comerciantes. Sin embargo, ambos eran solteros y eso había empezado a molestar a todo el mundo.

Un día, mientras comerciaban, una joven, Felicia, llamó la atención de Juan y éste la siguió hasta su casa. Quería saberlo todo sobre ella y empezó a hacer preguntas, pero no obtuvo respuestas. Le habló a Louis de la chica y éste prometió encontrar respuestas para John. Pero, a medida que Louis se acercaba a Felicia para encontrar respuestas, se enamoraron el uno del otro y decidieron casarse.

Cuando John se dio cuenta de lo que ocurría, decidió abandonar la ciudad y no se le volvió a ver.

FRIENDSHIPS AND LOVE

Carthage was one of the small cities in North Africa a long time ago, and in this city lived John and his friend, Louis. Both men were friends from childhood, as they were born a few days apart and grew up together as neighbours. Everyone knew them and over time, they began to look alike so much that people called them twins. Now, they had both grown up and become one of the Carthaginian traders, at a time when Carthago Nova became a major trading point that connected the Iberian peninsula to the wider Carthaginian trade network.

While John traded jewellery, Louis traded salts and together, they became rich traders. However, they both were unmarried and that had begun to bother everyone around.

One day, while trading, a young girl, Felicia caught John's eyes and he followed her home. He wanted to know everything about her and began to ask questions but he got no answers. He told Louis about the girl and he promised to find answers for John. But, as Louis moved closer to Felicia to find answers, they fell in love with each other and decided to get married. When John realised what was going on, he decided to leave the city and he was never seen again.

Vocabulary

Pequeño	Small
Comercio	Trade
Rico	Rich
Igual	Alike
Decidido	Decided
Preguntas	Questions
Infancia	Childhood
Comerciante	Trader
Ciudad	City
Mayor	Major
Creció	Grew
Gemelos	Twins
Juntos	Together

Comprehension Questions

¿Dónde vivían John y Louis? Where did John and Louis live?

¿Por qué eran amigos Juan y Luis? Why were John and Louis friends?

¿Por qué John abandonó la ciudad? Why did John leave the city?

Historical Note

When the Greeks, Phoenicians and Carthaginians entered the Iberian Peninsula, they contributed greatly to the development as they formed trading settlements. Carthago Nova (modern-day Cartagena) became a major Carthaginian trading hub, connecting the Iberian Peninsula to the broader Carthaginian trade network.

MARTHA Y BIG JOE

Una pareja, Martha y Big Joe vivían en la capital de Tartessos, en la época en que Tartessos era Rey. Estaban muy interesados en las artes y pintaban sobre la ropa para venderla a la gente. Cada día de mercado, llevaban estas ropas al mercado, las vendían a precios caros y volvían a casa antes del anochecer. La gente se preguntaba por su inusual manera de abandonar el mercado antes de tiempo sin importar lo mucho que hubieran vendido, así que empezaron a seguirlos a casa en secreto. Pero no descubrieron nada. La pareja volvía a casa cada tarde, pintaba toda la noche y vendía al día siguiente.

Con el tiempo, el número de personas que les compraban cuadros se fue reduciendo hasta que dejaron de tener clientes y su ropa se echó a perder. Cansada, Martha decidió pasear por la ciudad. Allí descubrió que la gente había empezado a pintar en la ropa como hacía ella con su marido, y las vendía a bajo precio.

De nuevo, ambas pensaron qué hacer para recuperar a sus clientes. Como ahora se utilizaba la escritura tartésica en los escritos de todo el mundo, decidieron pintar estos símbolos, algunos poco claros, en la ropa.

Así recuperaron a sus clientes y se hicieron más populares en el mercado.

MARTHA AND BIG JOE

A couple, Martha and Big Joe lived in the capital city of Tartessos, at the time when Tartessus was King. They were very interested in arts and would paint on clothes and sell to the people. Every market day, they would take these clothes to the market, sell them at expensive prices and go home before dusk. People wondered about their unusual manner of leaving the market early no matter how much they had sold, so people began to follow them home in secret. But they discovered nothing. The couple would walk home every evening, paint the whole night and sell the next day.

Over time, the number of people who bought paintings from them reduced until they no longer had customers and their clothes went to waste. Tired, Martha decided to walk around the city. There, she found out that people had started to paint on clothes like she did with her husband, and sold them at low prices.

Again, they both thought of what to do to get their customers back. Since the Tartessian script was now being used in writings all around, they decided to paint these symbols, some of which were unclear, in their clothes.

That way, they got their customers back and became more popular in the market.

Vocabulary

Pareja	Couple
Capital	Capital
Cansado	Tired
Poco claro	Unclear
Pinturas	Paintings
Tiempo	Time
Rey	King
Tarde	Evening
Mercado	Market
Día	Day
Caro	Expensive
Casa	Home
Ropa	Clothes

Comprehension Questions

¿A qué se dedicaban Martha y Gran Joe? What did Martha and Big Joe do for a living?

¿Por qué desconfiaba la gente de ellos? Why were the people suspicious of them?

¿Qué hicieron Martha y Gran Joe para recuperar a sus clientes? What did Martha and Big Joe do to regain their customers?

Historical Notes

The arrival of Phoenicians for trade and settlement brought about the development of writing in the peninsula. The Paleohispanic script was created and used before the advent of the latin script. The Tartessian script, an early writing system in the southwestern Iberian Peninsula, was used from the 8th to the 4th century BCE.

HIJO DE LA PROFECÍA

Mario era un niño profético. Aunque era bajito y corpulento, de niño varias personas le habían dicho que iba a crecer para ser fuerte e importante. Por eso, su madre le cuidaba especialmente. Lo bañaba ella misma y se aseguraba de que estuviera bien peinado. Los niños se burlaban de su estatura y él les contaba las profecías.

Se jactaba de que algún día llegaría a ser una gran persona. Esta desventaja llevó a su madre a asegurarse de que trabajara más que el resto de los chicos. No podía correr riesgos con su chico de las profecías. Estos valores que le impuso le hicieron destacar con el tiempo y pronto, cuando el antiguo líder de su colonia enfermó, nombró al joven Mario, de 17 años, nuevo líder de su colonia.

Mario no estaba satisfecho con la economía de su colonia y empezó a hablar con otros colonos griegos. Juntos crearon el Emporion en el siglo VI a.C., un puesto comercial central que los reunía a todos. También contribuyó a aumentar su riqueza, ya que se convirtió en un punto comercial clave donde se mezclaban diferentes culturas. Mario fue celebrado el resto de su vida por ello, cumpliendo finalmente las profecías, aunque la gente dice que su duro trabajo hizo la magia.

CHILD OF PROPHECY

Mario was a child of prophecy. Although short and stout, he had been told as a child by several people that he was going to grow up to be strong and important. This made his mother take special care of him. She took his bath herself and ensured that he was well groomed. The children around would make jest of his height and each time, he would tell them of the prophecies.

He would boast about how he would become a great person one day. This disadvantage led his mother to ensure that he worked harder than the rest of the boys. She couldn't take chances with her prophecy boy. These values she enforced on him stood him out over time and soon when the old leader of their colony became sick, he made the 17-year-old Mario the new leader of their colony.

Mario was unsatisfied with the economy of their settlement, and he began to speak with other Greek colonists. Together, they created the Emporion in the 6th century BCE, a central trading post which brought all of them together. It also helped build their wealth as it became a key trading post where different cultures mixed. Mario was celebrated for the rest of his life for this, finally fulfilling the prophecies, although people say his hard work did the magic.

Vocabulary

Corto	Short
Chico	Boy
Varios	Several
Fuerte	Strong
Profecía	Prophecy
Madre	Mother
Baño	Bath
Asegurar	Ensure
Alardear	Boast
Colonia	Settlement
Valores	Values
Economía	Economy

Comprehension Questions

¿Cómo cuidaba de él la madre de Mario? How did Mario's mother care for him?

¿Por qué Mario trabajaba más que los demás niños? Why did Mario work harder than other boys?

¿Qué hizo Mario por el acuerdo? What did Mario do for the settlement?

Historical Note

The arrival and settlement of archaic Greeks on the Iberian Peninsula saw the creation of Greek colonies. They named the peninsula Iberia, after the river Iber. Emporion, established by the Greeks in the 6th century BCE, became a key trading post, facilitating cultural exchange.

EL SOLDADO IMPECABLE

Darío era uno de los soldados del ejército cartaginés durante la Segunda Guerra Púnica. Era popular por sus bromas y su belleza. Los demás soldados querían saber cómo había vivido hasta entonces sin cicatrices del campo de batalla. Al comandante Aníbal le gustaba mucho Darío. Disfrutaba con las bromas de Darío y solía invitarle a su tienda cada vez que encontraban un lugar para descansar. Allí, Darius bromeaba sobre cómo había conocido a un hada que le había asegurado que seguiría siendo joven para siempre. Así pasaban el tiempo cada vez que encontraban lugares para descansar y encontraban humor en las malas condiciones.

Un día, Darío convocó a algunos hombres en Zama. Les informó de que el comandante le había pedido que le entregara algunos mensajes. Cuando todos llegaron al lugar de la reunión, Darío les dijo que sólo estaba bromeando y que no había ninguna reunión. Enfurecidos, los soldados empezaron a luchar contra él, pero al hacerlo fueron atacados y, como su defensa era débil, todos fueron capturados. Esto ayudó a sus enemigos a derrotarlos en Zama. Los pocos soldados que escaparon despidieron a Darío del ejército en honor a sus hermanos capturados.

THE FLAWLESS SOLDIER

Darius was one of the soldiers in the Carthaginian army during the Second Punic War. He was popular because of his jokes and beauty. The other soldiers wanted to know how he had lived so far without scars from the battlefield. The commander, Hannibal, was really fond of Darius. He enjoyed Darius' jokes and would often invite him to his tent whenever they found a place to rest. There, Darius would joke about how he had met a fairy who had assured him that he would remain young forever. This way, they passed time whenever they found places to rest and found humour in bad conditions.

One day, Darius called some of the men together in Zama. He sent information to them that the commander had asked him to deliver some messages. When they all got to the meeting ground, Darius told them that he was only joking and there was no meeting. In anger, the soldiers began to fight him but as they did this, they were attacked and since their defence was weak, they were all captured. This helped their enemies defeat them in Zama. The few soldiers that escaped sent Darius away from the army in honour of their captured brothers.

Vocabulary

Invitar	Invite
Cicatrices	Scars
Disfrutado	Enjoyed
Soldado	Soldier
Bromas	Jokes
Ejército	Army
Humor	Humour
Guerra	War
Hermano	Brother
Comandante	Commander
Cariñoso	Fond
Descanse	Rest

Comprehension Questions

¿Cómo se hicieron amigos Darío y el comandante? How did Darius and the commander become friends?

¿Por qué era popular Darío? Why was Darius popular?

¿Por qué lucharon los soldados contra Darío? Why did the soldiers fight Darius?

Historical Notes

The second punic war was fought between the Roman Republic and Carthage over control of the Iberian Peninsula. Eventually, the Romans came out Victorious and expelled the Carthaginians from the peninsula.

AMOR ANTIGUO

Augusto César, el emperador romano, era el marido de María. Lo conocía desde que eran niños y su amor había pasado de ser dos niños que jugaban juntos en la corte a adultos locos el uno por el otro. María era una mujer menuda de ojos dorados que cautivaban al emperador cada vez que ponía sus ojos en ella. Era tanta su distracción que pronto decidió no presentarse en la corte para asegurarse de que su marido tomaba las mejores decisiones sin distracciones.

Ahora bien, María era la persona favorita del emperador, pero ella misma no era una gran persona. Era grosera con todo el mundo excepto con su marido y a menudo le alababa por la expansión de la Hispania romana. Decía a todo el mundo que ella era su cerebro y que él no podía prescindir de ella.

Pronto, estos rumores llegaron al emperador y éste se enfureció. Pero por amor a ella, la llamó en privado y le advirtió asegurándose que le construiría un anfiteatro en la Emérita Augusta. Ella cambió inmediatamente y, cuando la Emerita Augusta se terminó en el año 25 a.C., fue la primera persona en utilizar el anfiteatro, una parte del proyecto que sirvió de muestra de la planificación urbanística romana.

OLD LOVE

Augustus Caesar, the Roman emperor, was Maria's husband. She had known him since they were kids and their love had grown from two young children who played together in courts to adults who were crazy about each other. Maria was a petite woman with golden eyes that wowed the emperor every time he set his eyes on her. She was so much of a distraction that she soon stopped going to court to ensure that her husband made the best decisions without distractions.

Now, Maria was the emperor's favourite person but she wasn't a great person herself. She was rude to everyone except her husband and would often praise him for the expansion of Roman Hispania. She told everyone around that she was his brain and he couldn't do without her.

Soon, these rumours reached the emperor and he was angered. But out of his love for her, he called her privately and warned her while assuring her that he would build her an amphitheatre in the Emerita Augusta. She changed immediately and when the Emerita Augusta was completed in 25 BCE, she was the first person to use the amphitheatre, a part of the project that showcased Roman urban planning.

Vocabulary

Ojos	Eyes
Mujer	Woman
Emperador	Emperor
En privado	Privately
Distracción	Distraction
Petite	Petite
Grosero	Rude
Marido	Husband
Dorado	Golden
Favorito	Favourite
Rumores	Rumours

Comprehension Questions

¿Por qué María era una distracción para el Emperador? Why was Maria a distraction to the Emperor?

¿Qué dijo María sobre el Emperador? What did Maria say about the Emperor?

¿Qué hizo cambiar a María? What made Maria change?

Historical Note

After taking control of the peninsula, the first thing the Romans did was to make the existing cities better. They also created more cities as a way of maximising the capacity of the peninsula. The economy grew as a result and Rome exported resources from the peninsula for its needs. Emerita Augusta (modern-day Mérida) was founded in 25 BCE, showcasing Roman urban planning, aqueducts, and an amphitheatre.

UNIDAD Y DECISIONES

Hace mucho tiempo, Adriano era carpintero cn la antigua ciudad de Roma. Aprendió de Juda, el carpintero borracho, y la gente de los alrededores esperaba que acabara siendo un borracho como su maestro. Sin embargo, demostró una gran dedicación a su oficio y pronto se hizo popular por sus diseños.

Viajó por todas partes para aprender más sobre el oficio, pero no se enamoró de la mayoría de las estructuras de viviendas que encontró, así que regresó a Roma y decidió acudir a otro maestro y aprender con esmero los entresijos de la construcción de estructuras de estilo romano, ya que se estaban haciendo populares en todo el mundo. Allí aprendió durante 3 años, tras los cuales se alejó de Roma y empezó a construir casas de estilo romano, al igual que los demás carpinteros.

Pronto conoció a Juan, un griego inteligente con mentalidad empresarial que se interesaba por la carpintería y el latín. Aunque la gente se había interesado más por la lengua, Adriano se sorprendió al ver lo aplicado que era Juan en el aprendizaje. Esto le llevó a enseñar a Juan el idioma y el oficio hasta que él también se convirtió en un experto. Se asociaron y pronto se convirtieron en unos de los carpinteros más ricos de su época.

UNITY AND DECISIONS

Adrian was a carpenter in the old city of Rome a long time ago. He learnt from Juda, the drunk carpenter and people around had expected that he would turn out a drunkard like his master. However, he showed great dedication to his craft and soon became popular for his designs.

He travelled far and wide to learn more about the trade of the business but he didn't fall in love with most of the other housing structures he found so he came back to Rome and decided to go to a different master and learn the intricacies of building Roman-style structures carefully since they were becoming popular all over the world. There, he studied for 3 years after which he moved away from Rome and began to build Roman-like houses, just like the other carpenters.

He soon met John, a smart business-minded Greek man who was interested in carpentry and Latin. Although people had become more interested in the language, Adrian was shocked to see how dedicated John was to learning. This led him to teach John the language and trade until he became an expert as well. They partnered and soon became some of the richest carpenters of their time.

Vocabulary

Borracho	Drunk
El más rico	Richest
Aprendido	Learnt
Maestro	Master
Artesanía	Craft
Viajado	Travelled
Carpintería	Carpentry
Conmocionado	Shocked
Experto	Expert
Amplio	Wide
Diseños	Designs

Comprehension Questions

¿Qué esperaba la gente que le pasara a Adrian? What did people expect would happen to Adrian?

¿Por qué regresó Adrián de sus viajes? Why did Adrian return from his travels?

¿Cómo ayudó Adrián a Juan? How did Adrian help John?

Historical Notes

Hispania was the name used for the Iberian Peninsula under Roman rule. The people were slowly culturally romanized and the local leaders became a part of the Roman aristocracy. Romanization influenced language, with Latin becoming prevalent, and architecture, with Roman-style structures dotting the landscape.

MIRA, ES LUKE

Lucas era muy amigo de San Osio de Córdoba, aunque se peleaban a menudo a causa de sus ideas opuestas. Mientras que el obispo se preocupaba mucho por las normas y la moral que guiaban el cristianismo, Lucas era más liberal y a menudo era la persona contraria en el consejo de Elvira, un equipo que tomaba decisiones sobre la moral y las costumbres cristianas. Este comportamiento de Lucas enfurecía a menudo a los demás miembros y muchas veces decidieron que ya no lo querían en el consejo. Pero el obispo se encargó de que todos le toleraran, como prueba de su destino.

El obispo pronto se cansó de los problemas de Lucas y le convocó a una reunión privada donde le rogó que abandonara el consejo, pero Lucas se mantuvo inflexible y empezó a hablar mal del obispo a todo el que le escuchaba. Pronto llegaron noticias a oídos del obispo y, de nuevo, llamó a Lucas para hablar con él. Pero a Lucas ya no le importaba. Abandonó la reunión y siguió difundiendo sus rumores.

Su caso no tardó en llegar al consejo de Elvira, que decidió apartarlo por completo del consejo para emitir un juicio justo. Cuando Luke se enteró de la noticia, se ahorcó en su habitación.

LOOK, IT'S LUKE

Luke was a very close friend of Saint Hosius of Córdoba although they fought often as a result of their opposing ideas. While the bishop cared a lot about the rules of Christianity, Luke was more liberal and was often the opposing person in the council of Elvira, a team that made decisions on Christian morality. This behaviour of Luke often angered the other members and they had decided that he was no longer wanted in the council many times. But the bishop ensured that they all tolerated him, as a test of their faith.

The Bishop soon became tired of Luke's troubles and called him to a private meeting where he was begged to leave the council but Luke was adamant and began to speak ill of the bishop to everyone who listened. News soon reached the bishop's ears and again, he called Luke to speak with him. But, Luke no longer cared. He walked out of the meeting and continued spreading his rumours.

His case was soon brought to the council of Elvira and they decided to remove him from the council completely to make a fair judgement. When Luke heard the news, he ran away from the city.

Vocabulary

Justo	Fair
Fe	Faith
Miembros	Member
Íntimo	Close
Enfadado	Angered
Obispo	Bishop
Obstinado	Adamant
Consejo	Council
Reglas	Rules
Reunión	Meeting
Eliminar	Remove

Comprehension Questions

¿Qué hizo el Consejo de Elvira? What did the Council of Elvira do?

¿Por qué los miembros estaban cansados de Luke? Why were the members tired of Luke?

¿Qué le ocurrió a Luke al final? What happened to Luke in the end?

Historical Notes

The Council of Elvira in Hispania addressed matters of Christian discipline, with canons on morality and ecclesiastical practices. Its purpose was to restore order and discipline in the church.

CASI AMOR

Fiera era popular en el antiguo Imperio Romano de Occidente por su valentía y belleza. Decía las cosas como las veía y atendía sus negocios con tanta gracia que era una de las comerciantes más ricas del imperio. Aunque muchos decían que su éxito se debía a lo bella que era, ella no se desanimaba y seguía viajando y comerciando por todas partes.

Un día, mientras comerciaba fuera de su ciudad, Fiera tuvo que pasar la noche en la capital para reunirse con algunos de sus amigos de la capital y discutir nuevas formas de mejorar sus negocios. Se alojó en una de las mejores casas de huéspedes y allí conoció a Theo, un amigo del emperador, Romulus Augustulus.

Habló con Theo durante toda la noche y la mañana siguiente, y al día siguiente hasta que pasó una semana entera en la capital. Le decía cosas que le aceleraban el corazón. Al octavo día, le pidió que la cortejara y decidieron que vendría a visitarla para su boda dentro de tres meses.

Desgraciadamente, nunca llegó, ya que Rómulo Augústulo fue depuesto dos meses después de su encuentro y Theo nunca volvió a aparecer.

ALMOST LOVE

Fiera was popular in the old Western Roman Empire for her courage and beauty. She said things the way she saw them and attended to her business with such grace that she was one of the rich traders in the empire. Although many said that she was successful because of how beautiful she was, she wasn't discouraged, she kept on travelling and trading all around.

While trading outside of her city one day, Fiera had to stay in the capital for the night so she could meet with some of her friends in the capital and discuss new ways to improve their business. She stayed in one of the best guest houses and there she met Theo, a friend of the emperor, Romulus Augustulus.

She spoke with Theo all through the night and the next morning, and the day after up until she had spent a full week in the capital. He said things that made her heart race. On the eighth day, she asked him to court her and they decided that he would come visit her for their wedding in three months. Alas, he never came as Romulus Augustulus was deposed two months after their meeting and Theo was never found again.

Vocabulary

Occidental	Western
Amigo	Friend
Valor	Courage
Gracia	Grace
Atender	Attend
Mejor	Best
Desanimado	Discouraged
Noche	Night
Invitado	Invited
Cortejar	Court
Boda	Wedding
Siguiente	Next
Visite	Visit

Comprehension Questions

¿Cómo se conocieron Fiera y Theo? How did Fiera and Theo meet?

¿Por qué Fiera era una comerciante de éxito? Why was Fiera a successful trader?

¿Qué hacía Fiera a menudo? What did Fiera do often?

Historical Notes

The fall of the Western Roman Empire in 476 CE marked the end of Roman Reign in Hispania, with Romulus Augustulus being deposed. After the fall, parts of Hispania came under the control of the Germanic tribes.

CARLA Y EL PÁJARO

Los francos eran una tribu germánica prominente en la antigua ciudad de Roma. Fueron algunas de las familias germanas más fuertes que entraron en el Imperio Romano y crearon reinos independientes, y una de ellas, el rey Carlomagno, llegó incluso a convertirse en el emperador del Sacro Imperio Romano Germánico años más tarde, tras la caída del Imperio Romano de Occidente.

Entre los miembros de esta tribu había un joven débil, Carla, que sufría epilepsia a menudo. Había sido separado de su antigua nodriza, que conocía las medicinas adecuadas para ayudarle con sus episodios, por lo que sus ataques se hicieron frecuentes. Pronto, los demás niños empezaron a dejarle fuera de sus reuniones sociales. Se negaban a permitirle asistir a cenas con ellos o sentarse a su mesa.

Carla se puso triste y lloraba mucho en su habitación. Mientras lloraba, un pájaro se posó junto a su ventana y le cantó. El pájaro tejió historias de amor para Carla y él sintió que algo vibraba en su cuerpo. Sorprendida, Carla siguió al pájaro hasta un arbusto y allí se encontró con un anciano que le dio de beber. Después, Carla se curó de epilepsia y los otros niños empezaron a jugar con él. Creció y se convirtió en un hombre fuerte y sano.

CARLA AND THE BIRD

The Franks were a large Germanic tribe in the old city of Rome. They were some of the strongest German families that entered the Roman Empire and created independent kingdoms and one of them, King Charlemagne even went on to become the Holy Roman Emperor years later after the fall of the Western Roman Empire.

Amongst the members of this tribe was a young weak boy, Carla, who suffered from seizures often. He had been separated from his old nurse who knew the right medication to give him, so his seizures happened often. Soon, the other children began to leave him out of their social gatherings. They refused to allow him to attend dinners with them or sit at their table.

Carla became sad and cried a lot in his room. While crying, a bird landed by his window and sang for him. The bird weaved tales of love for Carla and he felt something vibrate through his body. Surprised, Carla followed the bird to the bush and there, he met an old man who gave him some water to drink. After, Carla was healed of seizures and the other boys began to play with him. He grew up into a strong healthy man.

Vocabulary

Grandes	Large
Familias	Families
Permitir	Allow
Independiente	Independent
Cuentos	Tales
Saludable	Healthy
Débil	Weak
Beber	Drink
Separados	Separated
Enfermera	Nurse
Triste	Sad
Sucedió	Happened
Rechazado	Refused

Comprehension Questions

¿Por qué Carla tenía convulsiones frecuentes? Why did Carla have frequent seizures?

¿Por qué los otros niños dejaron de jugar con Carla? Why did the other boys stop playing with Carla?

¿Quién le hacía compañía? Who kept Carla's company?

Historical Notes

The end of the Western Roman Empire did not cause a total destruction of the Hispania civilization and society, although some institutions and infrastructure did decline. Germanic tribes, including Visigoths and Vandals, established their kingdoms, influencing local governance and culture. Spain's language, religion and the foundations of its laws started to take shape from this point in time.

RANDLE SIMONS

Randle Simons formaba parte de los visigodos en el siglo VIII y, para él, eso conllevaba mucho orgullo, ya que su pueblo gobernaba el reino más fuerte de Europa occidental. Su pueblo había saqueado Roma años antes y establecido el Reino Visigodo. Aunque no formaba parte de los miembros gobernantes, se enorgullecía de que su pueblo estuviera en el poder y a menudo se le encontraba tejiendo historias falsas sobre cómo era uno de los visigodos más importantes de la historia.

Hablaba de cómo una vez le habían enviado a luchar contra animales para que ellos también pudieran controlar el reino animal. Randle Simons contaba a la gente la pelea que tuvo con los leones y que le hizo perder dos dientes delanteros. Reunía a los niños por la noche y les contaba estas historias hasta que ya no quedaba ni rastro de luces. Después, acompañaba a los niños a casa y caminaba solo por el pueblo. Un día, mientras caminaba de noche, se encontró con Liv, una mujer que le desafió por sus cuentos y fanfarronadas. Enfadado por su atrevimiento, la retó a duelo.

Los niños les vieron batirse al día siguiente y, justo cuando estaba a punto de perder, desapareció y nunca más se le volvió a ver. Hoy se dice que se dejó llevar demasiado por sus mentiras y que su orgullo acabó con él.

RANDLE SIMONS

Randle Simons was part of the Visigoths in the 8th century and for him, that came with a lot of pride since his people ruled over the strongest kingdom in western Europe. His people had sacked Rome years before and established the Visigothic Kingdom. Although he wasn't a part of the ruling members, he still found pride in his people being in power and he would often be found weaving untrue tales about how he was one of the most important Visigoths ever.

He would talk about how he had once been sent to battle animals so they could control the animal kingdom as well. Randle Simons would tell people of the fight he had with the lions that made him lose two of his front teeth. He would gather children together at night and tell these tales until there was no longer any trace of lights. After this, he would escort the children home and walk through the town alone. One day, while walking in the night, he met Liv, a woman who challenged him over his tales and boasts. Angry at her audacity, he challenged her to a duel.

The children watched them fight the next day and after a long time, Randel Simons lost the duel. Liv made him confess to all his lies and promise to never tell lies again.

Vocabulary

Orgullo	Pride
Frente	Front
Reino	Kingdom
Destituido	Sacked
Establecido	Established
Poder	Power
Dientes	Teeth
Falso	Untrue
Animales	Animals
Controlar	Control
Leones	Lions
Duelo	Duel
Luz	Light

Comprehension Questions

¿Qué enorgullece a Randel Simons? What made Randel Simons proud?

¿Por qué se enfadó Randel Simons con Liv? Why was Randel Simons annoyed at Liv?

¿Qué ocurrió al final del duelo? What happened at the end of the duel?

Historical Notes

In the era of the Visigothic Kingdom, King Leovigild (c. 568–586) aimed to unite the Visigoths and Hispano-Romans and consolidate Visigothic power, emphasising religious unity.

SAHEED SUAVE

Hace mucho tiempo, Saheed fue uno de los jóvenes desplegados para unirse al ejército liderado por Tariq ibn Ziyad en la Batalla de Guadalete. A diferencia de los demás hombres, Saheed no estaba entrenado para la batalla y sólo estaba dispuesto porque amaba a Alá. Era un hombre blando y prefería quedarse en casa con su esposa, Shekinah, y su hijo de un año, Sheriff. Cuando supo la noticia de su despliegue, habló con su esposa y ella lo escondió detrás de su casa durante días.

Cada vez que los soldados venían a preguntar por él, ella se echaba al suelo y lloraba, culpando a todo el mundo de la desaparición de su marido. Lloraba tanto que los hombres acababan por dejarla en paz. Después, iba a ver a su marido. Sin que ellos lo supieran, el comandante había ordenado a algunos de los hombres que se quedaran vigilando la casa por si Saheed volvía. Saheed y Shekinah siguieron viviendo así durante un tiempo.

Un día, Saheed se cansó del escondite y decidió salir a tomar el aire. Los soldados lo vieron y lo capturaron de inmediato. Su mujer huyó con su hijo y, meses después, Saheed regresó tras la batalla a una casa vacía. Hasta su muerte, contó a menudo cómo el miedo destruyó su hogar.

SOFT SAHEED

A long time ago, Saheed was one of the young men sent to join the army led by Tariq ibn Ziyad in the Battle of Guadalete. Unlike all the other men, Saheed was not trained for battle and he was only willing because he loved Allah. He was a soft man and would prefer to stay home with his wife, Shekinah and his one-year-old son, Sheriff. When he heard the news of his deployment, he spoke to his wife and she hid him behind their home for days.

Each time the soldiers came to ask of him, she would fall to the ground and cry, blaming everyone for her husband's disappearance. She would cry so much that the men would eventually leave her alone. After, she would go see her husband. Unknown to them, the commander had ordered some of the men to stay behind and watch their home in case Saheed came back home. Saheed and Shekinah continued to live like this for a while.

One day, Saheed got tired of hiding and decided to come out for some air. The soldiers saw him and he was immediately captured. Afraid, his wife ran away with their son and months later, Saheed came back after the battle to an empty home. Until his death, he often told tales of how fear destroyed his home.

Vocabulary

Únase a	Join
Aire	Air
Miedo	Fear
Diferente de	Unlike
Enviado	Sent
Tierra	Ground
Grito	Cry
Entrenado	Trained
Suave	Soft
Prefiere	Prefer
Ordenado	Ordered
Observar	Watch

Comprehension Questions

¿Por qué Saheed no quería ir a la batalla? Why was Saheed unwilling to go to battle?

¿Cómo engañó la mujer de Saheed a los soldados? How did Saheed's wife deceive the soldiers?

¿Por qué huyó la mujer de Saheed de su casa? Why did Saheed's wife flee their home?

Historial Notes

The Muslim conquest of Hispania began in 711 CE, led by Tariq ibn Ziyad, resulting in the Battle of Guadalete. They defeated the Visigothic King Roderic and advanced rapidly into the peninsula, capturing major cities. Muslim rule expanded over the following decades and brought about important cultural, scientific and architectural contributions.

AMOR EN ESPINAS

Mark y Ahmed nacieron en uno de esos años en los que las batallas entre cristianos y musulmanes eran intensas. Los estados cristianos de los alrededores de su pequeña ciudad perseguían activamente a los musulmanes, ya que habían gobernado activamente en los últimos siglos. Fue en tiempos de Alfonso VI, una época terrible para que dos niños de religiones diferentes fueran amigos. El rey oprimía a los musulmanes que hasta entonces habían estado bajo su protección, así que los padres de Marcos y Ahmed intentaron que no se vieran mucho. Les contaban diferentes historias sobre cómo los gobernantes cristianos oprimían a los musulmanes para conseguir el poder, de modo que los niños se odiaban, pero esto hizo crecer el vínculo que tenían.

Como sus madres tampoco se querían mucho, impidieron que los niños se vieran y enfermaron. Después de una semana de cuidarlos individualmente sin ningún cambio significativo en su salud, las dos madres se reunieron y permitieron que los niños volvieran a jugar entre ellos. Mark y Ahmed se pusieron bien y, gracias a ello, las madres desarrollaron un vínculo en medio del caos que las rodeaba.

LOVE IN THORNS

Mark and Ahmed were born in one of those years when the battles between the Christians and Muslims were intense. The Christian states around their small town were fighting the Muslims for control and power. This was during the time of Alfonso VI, a bad time for two children from different religions to be friends. The king was oppressing Muslims who were previously under his protection at the time, so the parents of Mark and Ahmed tried to ensure they didn't see each other much. They told the boys different tales about how the Christian rulers were oppressing the Muslims to get power so the boys could hate each other but this grew the bond they had.

Since their mothers didn't like each other much as well, they stopped the boys from playing together and the boys fell sick. After a week of caring for them individually without any change in their health, the two mothers met up and allowed the children to play with each other again. Mark and Ahmed became well and through this, the mothers developed a bond amid the chaos around them.

Vocabulary

Nacido	Born
Ciudad	Town
Intenso	Intense
Siglos	Centuries
Protección	Protection
Cambiar	Change
Diferentes	Different
Gustar	Like
Individualmente	Individually
Bono	Bond
Enfermo	Sick
Entre	Between
Estados	States

Comprehension Questions

¿En qué periodo nacieron los niños? In what period were the boys born?

¿Por qué no se gustaban sus padres? Why did their parents dislike each other?

¿Pudieron los padres separar a los niños? Were the parents able to separate the boys?

Historical Notes

The Reconquista, a counter movement by Christians to retake Hispania, spanned centuries, with key battles like the Battle of Covadonga (c. 722) marking the beginning of Christian resistance.

LUCHA POR LA CORONA

El periodo comprendido entre 1475 y 1479 marcó una época importante para los pueblos de Portugal y Castilla. Dos de sus líderes, Juana la Beltraneja e Isabel I de Castillo, luchaban por la corona de Castilla y el pueblo estaba dividido sobre quién debía suceder a Enrique IV, el monarca fallecido. Mientras que Juana la Beltraneja era hija del difunto monarca, Isabel era su hermanastra. Ambas tenían vínculos con la corona y otros lugares, ya que se casaron con hombres poderosos también estratégicamente. Juana estaba casada con su tío, el rey Afonso V de Portugal, mientras que Isabel lo estaba con Fernando II de Aragón.

La batalla se prolongó durante años y ambos bandos reclamaron la victoria en diferentes momentos hasta la gran batalla de Toro. Aunque la batalla fue bastante indecisa, Fernando II fue lo suficientemente sabio como para enviar a otros lugares la noticia de que habían ganado, una decisión que hizo retroceder a los portugueses.

Isabel reafirmó su posición después de esto y aunque la lucha continuó durante años con ambos bandos ganando en diferentes posiciones, ella ya se había hecho cargo de Castilla. Finalmente, los portugueses se rindieron a cambio de un reparto favorable de algunos de los territorios en disputa.

FIGHT FOR THE CROWN

The period between 1475 and 1479 marked a significant time for the people of Portugal and Castille. Two of their leaders, Joanna 'la Beltraneja and Isabella I of Castillo were fighting for the crown of Castille and the people were divided on who was supposed to succeed Henry IV, the dead monarch. While Joanna 'la Beltraneja was the daughter of the late monarch, Isabella was his step-sister. They both had ties to the crown and other places as they married powerful men strategically as well. Joanna was married to her uncle, King Afonso V of Portugal while Isabella was married to Ferdinand II of Aragon.

The battle went on for years with both sides claiming victory at different points until the great Battle of Toro. Although the battle was quite indecisive, Ferdinand II was wise enough to send words to other places that they had won, a decision that made the Portugals step back.

Isabella went on to reaffirm her position after this and although the fight continued for years with both sides winning at different positions, she had already taken charge of Castille. The Portugals finally surrendered in return for a favourable share of some of the territories being disputed.

Vocabulary

Periodo	Period
Personas	People
Significativo	Significant
Hija	Daughter
Lazos	Ties
Corona	Crown
Lugares	Places
Años	Years
Lados	Lados
Ganado	Won
Territorios	Territories
Grande	Great

Comprehension Questions

¿Cuál fue la causa de la disputa entre Castilla y Portugal? What caused the dispute between Castille and Portugal?

¿Qué relación tenían Joana e Isabel con Enrique IV? How were Joana and Isabella related to Henry IV?

¿Quién ganó las batallas? Who won the battles?

Historical Notes

The War of Castilian Succession was a conflict between the supporters of Isabella 1 of Castile and Joana lá Beltraneja. Isabella was a niece to the dead King Henry IV while Isabella was his daughter. The war lasted from 1475 to 1479 after which Isabella was recognised as the legitimate queen.

ADOLESCENTES AMBICIOSOS

Isabel I de Castilla, hermanastra de Enrique IV de Castilla, y Fernando II de Aragón, heredero de Juan II de Aragón, eran ambos adolescentes cuando se conocieron en 1469. Aunque adolescentes, eran inteligentes y políticamente listos. Sabían que ambos querían la Corona de Castilla y decidieron luchar conjuntamente por ella. Eran lo suficientemente inteligentes como para saber que trabajar juntos sería mejor para ellos a pesar de que Isabel tenía 18 años y Fernando sólo 17. A la semana de conocerse, se casaron.

A menudo paseaban juntos mientras discutían ideas aleatorias sobre Castilla y sobre cómo derrotar a Juana, la sobrina adoptiva de Isabel que también reclamaba la corona de Castilla. Cuando comenzó la batalla entre Isabel y Juana tras la muerte de Enrique, trabajaron juntas, lo que les llevó a la victoria y a la unificación de España, aunque gobernaron los dos reinos de forma independiente.

Siempre que pasaban tiempo juntas, hablaban de la fe católica y se mostraban muy vehementes con la gente de sus cortes. En 1494 fueron nombrados Reyes Católicos por el Papa y organizaron una gran fiesta para celebrar sus nuevos títulos.

Se trata de una adaptación ficticia de la historia de Isabel I y Fernando II.

AMBITIOUS TEENAGERS

Isabella I of Castille, the step-sister of Henry IV of Castille and Ferdinand II of Aragon, heir apparent of Juan II of Aragon were both teenagers when they met in 1469. Although teenagers, they were smart and politically sound. They knew that they both wanted the Crown of Castille and decided to jointly fight for it. They were intelligent enough to know that working together would be better for them even though Isabella was 18 and Ferdinand was only 17. Within a week of meeting each other, they got married.

They would often take walks together while discussing ideas about Castille and how to defeat Joanna, Isabella's step-niece who also had a claim to the crown of Castille. When the battle between Isabella and Joanna began after Henry's death, they worked together, leading to their victory and unification of Spain, although they ruled the two kingdoms independently.

Whenever they spent time together, they would discuss the Catholic faith and be very vocal about the church with people of their courts. They were eventually named the Catholic King and Queen in 1494 by the pope and they threw a big party to celebrate their new titles.

This is a fictional adaptation of the story of Isabella I and Ferdinand II.

Vocabulary

Adolescentes	Teenagers
Títulos	Titles
Inteligente	Smart
Políticamente	Politically
Celebrar	Celebrate
Conjuntamente	Jointly
Paseos	Walks
Ideas	Ideas
Reclamacíon	Claim
Victoria	Victory
Unificación	Unification
Discutir	Discuss
Fiesta	Party

Comprehension Questions

¿Qué unió a Isabel y Fernando? What brought Isabella and Ferdinand together?

¿De qué hablaban a menudo? What did they often discuss?

¿Lograron vencer a Joana? Did they succeed in defeating Joana?

Historical Notes

The Catholic Monarchs, Isabella I of Castile and Ferdinand II of Aragon, married in 1469, unifying Castile and Aragon under joint rule. Their marriage led to the foundation of the unification of Spain.

FERVENT ABDUL

Abdul era uno de los judíos que vivían en España cuando Isabel I y Fernando II gobernaban el reino. Era musulmán desde muy joven y nunca ocultó su religión a nadie. Allá donde iba, hablaba de Alá y de lo misericordioso que era su Dios. Pero las cosas tuvieron que cambiar cuando Isabel y Fernando llegaron al poder, ya no podía hablar de Alá como antes. El Reino se había vuelto hostil hacia musulmanes y judíos y cada nuevo mes solía ser testigo de las políticas que oprimían a musulmanes y judíos.

Mientras la comunidad cristiana y el Papa elogiaban a Isabel y Fernando siempre que podían por su valentía y su fe, a Abdul le molestaban estas mismas cosas. Una vez a la semana, se quedaba en casa todo el día para rezar por otros musulmanes como él, pero nada mejoraba.

Abdul se desanimó tanto que un día salió a la calle y habló de Alá a todo el que veía, sin importarle las consecuencias. Fue arrestado y llevado ante los monarcas. Éstos dictaron el decreto de que los judíos debían convertirse al catolicismo en cuatro meses o abandonar España, y liberaron a Abdul. Un mes después se trasladó a Portugal.

Se trata de una adaptación ficticia de los acontecimientos que pudieron conducir al decreto de la Alhambra en 1492.

FERVENT ABDUL

Abdul was one of the Muslims who lived in Spain when Isabella I and Ferdinand II ruled the kingdom. He had been a Muslim from a young age and he never hid his religion from anyone. Wherever he went, he would talk about Allah and how merciful his God was. But things needed to change when Isabella and Ferdinand came into power, he could no longer talk about Allah like he used to. The Kingdom had become hostile towards Muslims and Jews and each new month would usually witness the policies that oppressed the Muslims and Jews.

While the Christian community and the pope praised Isabella and Ferdinand as often as possible for their bravery and faith, Abdul was bothered by these same things. Once a week, he would stay home all through the day to pray for other Muslims like him yet nothing was improving.

Abdul became so discouraged that one day, he went into the streets and talked about Allah to everyone he saw, without care for the consequences. He was arrested and brought before the monarchs. They issued the decree that Jews should convert to Catholicism in four months or leave Spain, and released Abdul. He moved to Portugal a month later.

This is a fictional adaptation of events that could have led up to the Alhambra decree in 1492.

Vocabulary

Edad	Age
Políticas	Politics
Sin	Without
Religión	Religion
Jóvenes	Young
Calles	Streets
Liberados	Released
Cuidar	Care
Elogiado	Praised
Nunca	Never
Hostil	Hostile
Testigo	Witness

Comprehension Questions

¿Qué hacía Abdul allá donde iba? What did Abdul do wherever he went?

¿Por qué se desanimó Abdul? Why was Abdul discouraged?

¿Qué le ocurría a Abdul cuando hablaba de Alá a la gente? What happened to Abdul when he talked about Allah to people?

Historical Notes

The Alhambra Decree issued by Isabella I and Ferdinand II in 1492 ordered the expulsion of Jews and Muslims from Hispania, leading to significant demographic changes. It was seen as a continuation of the reconquista, with muslims and jews given the option to convert and be allowed to stay. However, the converts were later expelled as well.

ODIO A UNO MISMO

Hace mucho tiempo, Pierre II era uno de los hombres que navegaban con Jean de Béthencourt, el explorador francés, cuando éste se encontraba en la expedición a las Islas Canarias. A menudo se le llamaba Pierre II porque había otro Pierre entre los hombres que era sacerdote. La mayoría de los hombres que navegaban eran viejos amigos de Jean que entendían sus objetivos y estaban interesados en cumplir sus sueños, pero para Pierre, su motivación era diferente. Odiaba a Jean desde hacía mucho tiempo y estaba deseando verle fracasar. No le importaba perder la vida en el proceso.

Se había despreocupado tanto de la vida que lo único que le importaba era el fracaso de su antiguo enemigo. Los otros hombres a su alrededor pensaban que él se preocupaba por ellos, así que le contaban los planes que Jean había hecho con algunos de ellos. Cada vez, él intentaba por todos los medios destruir los planes. Pronto, Jean se hizo más amigo de Pierre y discutió sus planes con él, pero se dio cuenta de que cada plan que discutía con Pierre a menudo fracasaba. Pronto dejó de hablar con Pierre después de que se apoderaran de la isla de Lanzarote. Por odio a sí mismo, Pierre se suicidó por la victoria.

SELF HATE

Long ago, Pierre II was one of the men who sailed with Jean de Béthencourt, the French Explorer when he was on the expedition to the Canary Islands. He was often called Pierre II because there was another Pierre amongst the men who was a priest. Most of the men who sailed were old friends of Jean who understood his goals and were interested in fulfilling his dreams but for Pierre, his motivation was different. He had hated Jean for the longest time and was looking forward to seeing him fail. He didn't mind losing his life in the process.

He had become so unbothered about life that all he cared about was the failure of his long-time enemy. The other men around him thought he cared about them, so they would tell him about the plans Jean made with some of them. Each time, he would try his best to destroy the plans. Soon, Jean became closer to Pierre and would discuss his plans with him but he noticed that every plan he discussed with Pierre often fell through. He soon stopped speaking with Pierre after they took over the Island of Lanzarote. Out of self-hate, Pierre killed himself over the victory.

Vocabulary

Despreocupado	Unbothered
Navegado	Sailed
Explorador	Explorer
Sacerdote	Priest
Entre	Amongst
Metas	Goals
Sueño	Dream
Motivación	Motivation
Fracaso	Fail
Odiado	Hated
Proceso	Process
Vida	Life
Enemigo	Enemy
Destruir	Destroy

Comprehension Questions

¿Por qué Pierre navegó con Jean? Why did Pierre sail with Jean?

¿Por qué Jean dejó de confiar en Pierre? Why did Jean stop confiding in Pierre?

¿Cómo le afectó al final el odio de Pierre? How did Pierre's hatred affect him in the end?

Historical Questions

The conquest of the Canary Islands (1402–1496) involved European explorers like Jean de Béthencourt, leading to the incorporation of the islands into the Crown of Castile. Initially, the indigenous people of the Island resisted external domination. However, they were greatly weakened by the diseases and plagues brought by the Europeans into their society and the use of superior weaponry by the Europeans led to the native's eventual defeat and subjugation. Afterwards, the Islands became a part of the Crown of Castile.

POR EL AMOR DE EMILY

Cristóbal Colón fue un explorador popular hace mucho tiempo, pero un detalle importante que la gente desconocía era su joven novia, Emily, a la que había amado años antes de empezar a explorar el mundo, antes de perder a su esposa. Emily era una mujer a la que le encantaba viajar. Le interesaban los lugares nuevos y la belleza que ofrecían. Hablaba de esos lugares con tanto deleite que cualquiera estaría dispuesto a patrocinar su viaje. Pero había un problema, Emily no podía caminar y él no podía casarse con ella.

Había nacido con malas piernas y se pasaba el día sentada. Pero cada vez que Christopher la visitaba, ella hablaba de sus sueños con él. Juntos planeaban viajes en sus cabezas. Estas conversaciones animaron a Christopher a dedicarse a la exploración. Quería ver el mundo que Emily tanto amaba. Quería ver esos lugares para poder volver y contárselos a ella. Emily se alegró mucho cuando los Reyes Católicos decidieron patrocinar sus viajes.

Después de descubrir América durante su viaje en 1492, volvió con Emily, pero ella había muerto de gripe. Juró no volver a casarse y después tomó una amante.

FOR THE LOVE OF EMILY

Christopher Columbus was a popular explorer a long time ago but an important detail people didn't know about was his young sweetheart, Emily who he had loved years before he began to explore the world, before he lost his wife. Emily was a woman who loved to travel. She was interested in new places and the beauty they offered. She would talk of these places with such delight that anyone would be willing to sponsor her trip. But there was an issue, Emily couldn't walk and he couldn't marry her.

She was born with bad legs and she sat all day long. But each time Christopher visited her, she spoke of her dreams with him. They planned voyages in their heads together. These discussions encouraged Christopher to take up exploring. He wanted to see the world Emily loved so much. He wanted to see these places so he could come back and tell her all about them. Emily was so happy when the Catholic monarchs decided to sponsor his journeys.

After he discovered the Americans during his voyage in 1492, he came back to Emily but she had died of the flu. He vowed not to marry again and took a mistress after.

Vocabulary

Detalle	Detail
Cariño	Sweetheart
Patrocinar	Sponsor
Acerca de	About
Comenzó	Began
Mundo	World
Ofrecido	Offered
Deleite	DElight
Dispuesto	Willing
Viajes	Voyages
Alentado	Encouraged

Comprehension Questions

¿Qué le gustaba a Emily? What did Emily love?

¿De qué hablaron Christopher y Emily juntos? What did Christopher and Emily discuss together?

¿Por qué Christopher se hizo explorador? Why did Christopher become an explorer?

Historical Notes

Columbus's first voyage in 1492, sponsored by the Catholic Monarchs, marked the encounter with the Americas, initiating European exploration and colonisation.

EL ACHE

Martin fue uno de los hombres con los que se comerciaba a través del Océano Atlántico con destino a España en el siglo XVII. Fue intercambiado por productos manufacturados de África y trabajó en una plantación de azúcar durante años. Fue intercambiado junto a su mujer, Dorcas, y tuvo que dejar a su anciana madre en casa. Esto le enfadaba mucho y nunca sonreía. Los otros esclavos se burlaban a menudo de él, pero nunca reaccionaba.

No sabía adónde habían llevado a su mujer y la veía a menudo en sueños. En esos sueños, ella lloraba y le suplicaba que la ayudara, pero él no podía hacer nada. Su duro trabajo pronto hizo que su amo le conociera y a menudo le invitaba a pasear con él. Mientras paseaba, su amo le contaba cosas de su vida y pronto Martin aprendió la lengua de su amo. Esto alegró al amo de Martin y lo convirtió en el jefe de los demás esclavos. Sin embargo, Martin era un hombre infeliz.

Se entristecía con el paso de los años y un día se suicidó de una puñalada. Su amo enterró a Martin en su propia casa y dejó de aceptar nuevos esclavos tras su muerte, pero nunca liberó a los antiguos.

THE ACHE

Martin was one of the men who was traded across the Atlantic Ocean to Spain in the 17th century. He was exchanged for manufactured goods from Africa and worked in a sugar plantation for years. He was traded alongside his wife, Dorcas and had to leave his old mother at home. This greatly angered him and he never smiled. The other slaves would often tease him but he never reacted.

He didn't know where his wife had been traded to and he saw her in his dreams often. In those dreams, she would cry and beg him to help her but he was helpless himself. His hard work soon made his master know him and he would often be invited to join the man on walks. While walking, his master would tell him about his life and soon enough, Martin learned the language of his master. This gladdened Martin's master and he made Martin the head of the other slaves. Yet, Martin was an unhappy man.

He became sadder as the years passed and one day, he stabbed himself to death. His master buried Martin in his own home and stopped taking new slaves after his death, but never released the old ones.

Vocabulary

En	Across
Ayuda	Help
Océano	Ocean
Junto a	Alongside
Sonrisa	Smile
Esclavos	Slaves
Desamparados	Helpless
Infeliz	Unhappy
Más triste	Sadder
Enterrados	Buried
Intercambiados	Exchanged
Tease	Tease

Comprehension Questions

¿Por qué Martin nunca fue feliz? Why was Martin never happy?

¿Por qué le caía bien al amo de Martin? Why did Martin's master like him?

¿Qué ocurrió tras la muerte de Martin? What happened as a result of Martin's death?

Historical Notes

The Manila-Acapulco Galleon Trade (1565–1815) connected Asia, the Americas, and Europe, significantly influencing global trade but also causing negative cultural and economic impacts to the regions involved and a lot of benefits to Europe. It used forced labour from the subjugated region and traded their resources such as silk, spices and porcelain to Europe.

PIERRE

Todos los que conocían a Pierre sabían que era un escritor fracasado. Hablaba a menudo de sus libros, pero nadie los veía nunca. Incluso hablaba de cómo sus libros habían llegado a las librerías, pero nadie veía sus libros en ninguna parte. Empezaba a parecer que mentía para llamar la atención. Algunos días, decía a la gente que era amigo de Miguel de Cervantes, el gran escritor, y que había influido en sus libros. Pronto, la gente empezó a rehuirle y nadie quiso volver a escuchar sus mentiras.

Un día, su vecino le dijo que Miguel iba a llegar al pueblo y que le encantaría que Pierre le presentara al autor cuyos libros florecieron. Lo había dicho para deshonrar a Pierre, pero éste había ideado un plan. Se adelantó a su vecino, llevando consigo su obra. Se reunió con Miguel en la biblioteca y le mostró su obra. Miguel quedó impresionado y decidió escribir un libro con Pierre.

Cuando el vecino de Pierre los vio juntos, se lo contó a todo el mundo y Pierre pronto volvió a ser popular y finalmente publicó sus libros. Pero nunca trabajó con Miguel por miedo a no ser lo bastante bueno.

PIERRE

Everyone who knew Pierre knew he was a failed writer. He often talked of his books but no one ever saw any of them. He would even talk about how his books had made it into bookstores yet no one saw his books anywhere. He had begun to look like he was lying for attention. Some days, he would tell people that he was friends with Miguel de Cervantes, the great writer and he had influenced his books. Soon, the people began to shun him and no one wanted to listen to his lies again.

One day, his neighbour told him that Miguel was coming into town and he would love Pierre to introduce him to the author whose books flourished. He had said this to disgrace Pierre but Pierre had devised a plan. He went ahead of his neighbour, taking along with him his work. He met with Miguel at the library and showed him his work. Miguel was impressed and decided to write a book with Pierre.

When Pierre's neighbour saw them together, he told everyone about it and Pierre soon became popular again and finally published his books. But, he never worked with Miguel out of fear that he wasn't good enough.

Vocabulary

Escritor	Writer
Atención	Attention
Libros	Books
Mentira	Lying
Influenciado	Influenced
Evitar	Shun
Escuchar	Listen
Desgracia	Disgrace
Ideado	Devised
Suficiente	Enough
Adelante	Ahead
A lo largo de	Along

Comprehension Questions

¿Por qué la gente rehuía a Pierre? Why did people shun Pierre?

¿Cómo se hizo Pierre popular? How did Pierre become popular?

¿Por qué Pierre nunca escribió un libro con Miguel? Why did Pierre never write a book with Miguel?

Historical Notes

Spanish conquistadors, including Hernán Cortés and Francisco Pizarro, played crucial roles in the conquest of major American civilizations. It allowed the imperial power of Spain to exploit the Americas for resources, thereby monopolising trade across the Atlantic and enriching its economy.

AMOR Y AMBICIONES

Tras la muerte del soberano de los Habsburgo en España, Marta, sastra de profesión, regresa a España con su marido, Juan. Ambos se habían trasladado fuera del país a una edad temprana con sus padres y habían crecido juntos en las afueras. Tenían 9 años cuando sus padres hicieron las maletas un miércoles por la noche y atravesaron pueblos hasta llegar al pueblecito donde vivían. Como los dos eran los únicos niños que había, era normal que se hicieran tan amigos que se casaran sin importarse mucho el uno del otro. Llevaban diez años casados y, cuando se enteraron de que el soberano de los Habsburgo había muerto, se llevaron a sus dos hijos, Ana y Brígida, para reclamar también una parte del trono.

Cuando llegaron a la capital, se alojaron en una posada la primera noche e hicieron averiguaciones sobre el palacio y los acontecimientos de los alrededores. Se entrevistaron con algunas personas y finalmente consiguieron a alguien que podía ponerse en contacto con el duque de Marlborough. A la mañana siguiente, se entrevistaron con el duque, quien inmediatamente les dijo que no tenían ningún derecho y les aconsejó que abandonaran la ciudad, ya que existía la posibilidad de una guerra debido a la falta de un sucesor claro. Juan decidió que debían marcharse inmediatamente para evitar verse atrapados en la guerra, ya que no tenían derecho directo al trono. El padre de John era primo del soberano fallecido, pero como los padres ya no vivían y la familia llevaba demasiado tiempo fuera, no tenían a nadie que respaldara sus reclamaciones. Sin embargo, Martha estaba demasiado obsesionada con el trato que conllevaba la realeza, así que convenció a John de que debían quedarse atrás y ver si podían formar una unión con alguna de las otras personas que tenían derecho directo al trono. Decidieron reunirse de nuevo con el duque, pero éste no les escuchó más de cinco minutos antes de marcharse enfadado.

Ahora, Juan se había cansado de las ambiciones de su esposa y empezó a quedarse en la posada con los niños mientras Marta se dedicaba a formar alianzas. Entabló amistad con Ruth, el ama de llaves, y se pasaba el día hablando con ella. Poco a poco, se fue enamorando de esta mujer tranquila que le hacía sentir como de la realeza más que Martha. Cuando Martha descubrió su floreciente relación con Ruth, cogió a sus hijos y se marchó de la ciudad. Meses después, Ruth también echó a John y éste perdió todo lo que poseía.

LOVE AND AMBITIONS

After the death of the Habsburg ruler in Spain, Martha, a tailor, moved back to Spain with her husband, John. They had both moved out of the country at a young age with their parents and had grown up together on the outskirts. They were 9 when their parents packed one Wednesday night and moved across towns until they got to the small village where they lived. Now, since these two were the only children around as they grew, it was only normal that they became so close that they got married without caring much for each other. Now, they had been married for 10 years and when they heard that the Habsburg ruler was dead, they took their two children, Anna and Bridget with them in a bid to claim a part of the throne as well.

When they got into the capital, they lodged into an inn the first night and made enquiries about the palace and the happenings around. They met with some of the people and finally got someone who could contact the Duke of Marlborough. The next morning, they met with the Duke who immediately told them they had no claim at all and advised them to leave town as there was a possibility of a war due to the lack of a clear successor. John decided that they needed to leave immediately to prevent being caught up in the war since they didn't have a direct claim to the throne. John's father were cousins of the dead ruler but since the parents were no longer alive and the family had been away for too long, they had no one to back their claims. But, Martha was too obsessed with the treatment that came with royalty, so she convinced John that they needed to stay back and see if they could form a union with any of the other people who had direct claim to the throne. They decided to meet with the Duke again but he didn't listen to them for more than five minutes before leaving in anger.

Now, John had become tired of his wife's ambitions and began to stay back in the inn with the children while Martha went about forming alliances. He developed a friendship with Ruth, the housekeeper and would talk to her all day. Slowly, he fell in love with this quiet woman who made him feel like royalty more than Martha ever did. When Martha discovered his blooming relationship with Ruth, she took her children and left town. Months later, Ruth sent John away as well and he lost everything he owned.

Worldwide Nomad

Vocabulary

Muerte	Death
Gobernante	Ruler
Sastre	Tailor
País	Country
Padre	Parent
Noche	Night
En	Around
Niños	Children
Reclamación	Claim
Capital	Capital

Comprehension Questions

¿A qué se dedica Martha? What is Martha's occupation?

¿A qué edad se fueron del país los padres de Marta? At what age did Martha's parents move out of the country?

¿Por qué se quedó Juan en la posada con los niños? Why did John stay back in the inn with the children?

Historical Note

The war of Spanish Succession took place due to the lack of a clear successor to the Spanish throne after the death of the last Habsburg ruler, leading to a European-wide conflict. Figures like Louis XIV of France and the Duke of Marlborough were key players. It was triggered by the lack of a clear successor to the Spanish throne after the death of the last Habsburg ruler, leading to a European-wide conflict.

CÍRCULO DE LA VIDA

Paul nació católico, de padres que practicaban el culto casi siempre y se encontraban a menudo en la iglesia. Creció en las doctrinas de la iglesia católica y estaba profundamente interesado en ser padre, como su tío Lucas. Sin embargo, a medida que crecía, no podía dejar de notar las diferencias en las doctrinas de la iglesia católica y la de los protestantes que seguían la creencia de la Reforma Protestante. Aunque estas diferencias no importaban cuando era pequeño, pronto empezaron a importar cuando los protestantes empezaron a ganar terreno y estallaron una serie de guerras entre los protestantes y la iglesia católica. Mientras que se creía que los protestantes iniciaron el movimiento debido a los abusos en la iglesia católica, la iglesia católica, según los padres de Paul, los veía como gente tonta que quería destruir la iglesia.

Como a Paul le fascinaba la Biblia, le resultó fácil creer en la superioridad de la Biblia, al igual que los protestantes, y muy pronto sus padres empezaron a darse cuenta de que se estaba acercando a la creencia de los protestantes. Tuvieron tanto miedo de que la gente se enterara, que encerraron a Pablo en casa y le enseñaron las doctrinas de la iglesia católica por todas partes. Pero Pablo era terco. Los castigos endurecieron su creencia en el movimiento protestante. Sus padres decidieron llevarlo al cura, que rezó durante días sobre él hasta que decidió cambiar de creencias. Al cuarto día, Paul se cansó de las oraciones y cedió a sus exigencias. Dejó de hablar del movimiento protestante y permaneció más tiempo en la iglesia.

Al cabo de un año, sus padres decidieron que era hora de que empezara a formarse para ser sacerdote y lo llevaron a la iglesia. Allí le querían todos. El cura le llevaba a actos y juntos predicaban a la gente. Pronto se hizo popular entre los demás estudiantes.

Un día, el cura envió a Pablo a buscar material al pueblo de al lado. Allí conoció a Evelyn, una joven protestante. Al verla, Paul se sintió atraído por su brillante carácter y pronto tuvo claro que lo único que quería era pasar el resto de su vida con ella. Le contó lo que sentía por ella y, cuando supo que ella sentía lo mismo, renunció a su sacerdocio y se casó con ella. Sus padres dejaron de hablarle y por fin encontró la libertad para volver a unirse al movimiento protestante.

CIRCLE OF LIFE

Paul was born a Catholic to parents who worshiped almost every time and were often found in the church. He grew in the doctrines of the Catholic church and was deeply interested in being a father, after his uncle, Lucas. However, as he grew, he couldn't but notice the differences in the doctrines of the Catholic church and that of the Protestants who followed the belief of the Protestant Reformation. While these differences didn't matter as a young child, they soon began to matter when the protestants began to gain ground and a series of wars broke out between the protestants and the Catholic church. While the protestants were believed to start the movement due to the abuses in the Catholic church, the Catholic church according to Paul's parents saw them as silly people who wanted to destroy the church.

Since Paul was fascinated with the Bible, it was easy for him to believe in the superiority of the Bible, just like the protestants and soon enough, his parents began to notice that he was moving towards the belief of the protestants. They became so afraid that people would know, so they would lock Paul in the house and teach him the doctrines of the Catholic church all over. But Paul was stubborn. The punishments hardened his belief in the Protestant movement. His parents decided to take him to the priest who prayed for days over him until he decided to change his beliefs. By the fourth day, Paul was tired of the prayers and he gave in to their demands. He stopped speaking of the Protestant movement and stayed in church more.

After a year, his parents decided that it was time for him to begin training to be a priest and took him to the church. There, he was loved by everyone. The priest took him out to events and together, they would preach to people. He soon became popular amongst the other students.

One day, the priest sent Paul to get some materials in the next town. There, he met a young lady, Evelyn who was a Protestant. When Paul saw the lady, he was drawn to her bright nature and it soon became clear to him that all he wanted to do was spend the rest of his life with her. He told her how he felt about her and when he found out she felt the same way, he renounced his priesthood and married her. His parents stopped speaking to him and he finally found the freedom to join the Protestant movement again.

Vocabulary

Nacido	Born
Adorado	Worshiped
Casi	Almost
A menudo	Often
Padre	Father
Tío	Uncle
Creencia	Belief
Diferencia	Difference
Ganar	Gain
Movimiento	Movement
Tonto	Silly
Fascinado	Fascinated

Comprehension Questions

¿Por qué Paul creía que su religión era superior? Why did Paul think his religion was superior?

¿Por qué Paul se sentía atraído por Evelyn? Why was Paul drawn to Evelyn?

¿Cuál era la religión de los padres de John? What was the religion of John's parents?

Historical Note

The Wars of Religion were marked by conflicts between Catholic and Protestant states across Europe, including the Thirty Years' War. The Portuguese Empire expanded through exploration, while the Wars of Religion (e.g., the Thirty Years' War) involved conflicts between Catholic and Protestant states in Europe.

UN HOMBRE CON VOLUNTAD

Louis era uno de esos hombres que creían en el libre pensamiento y no le interesaba que la gente le dijera lo que tenía que hacer. Creía que todos los hombres tenían derecho a elegir en quién querían creer, y esto le trajo problemas muchas veces. Siempre se apresuraba a regañar a la gente y a mencionar lo estúpidos que creía que eran todos. Voltaire y Rousseau escribieron algunos de sus libros favoritos y no podía mantener una simple conversación sin mencionar sus nombres. Era la época en que la mayoría de las editoriales publicaban libros que promovían la ciencia y la razón, así que no era de extrañar que le gustaran estos libros, ya que los escritores eran populares. Sin embargo, su obsesión era cada vez más extraña y la gente de su entorno ya no podía conversar con él correctamente. Parecía inestable y siempre estaba diciendo cosas que parecían poco razonables.

Cansado de las críticas de todos los que le rodeaban, Louis decidió abrir una pequeña editorial para poder ayudar a que la gente que escribía cosas que le gustaban llegara a un público más amplio. Utilizó todos sus ahorros y pidió préstamos para poner en marcha esta editorial que todo el mundo le había desaconsejado. Durante el primer mes, buscó escritores, filósofos y científicos a los que pudiera publicar y no encontró a ninguno. Envió noticias a las asociaciones, pero nadie estaba dispuesto a confiar en su pequeña empresa. Abatido, cerró brevemente la empresa durante dos semanas. Durante este tiempo, anotó los nombres de algunas de las personas con las que quería trabajar y les envió cartas solicitándoles sus manuscritos. Volvió a abrir la empresa y envió notas, pero no consiguió nada. La gente empezó a insultar su lógica empresarial y le recordaron las veces que les había llamado estúpidos. Para demostrarles que estaban equivocados, Louis recopiló manuscritos sobre cosas que no le interesaban y los publicó. Ninguno de los libros vendió más de cinco ejemplares cada uno y ni siquiera Louis pudo leerlos. A pesar de todo, seguía enviando cartas a las personas cuyos manuscritos quería.

Al tercer mes de abrir Louis, los acreedores empezaron a molestarle. Visitaron su casa y amenazaron con arrestarle si no pagaba inmediatamente. La gente le aconsejó que vendiera la editorial para reunir el dinero necesario, pero él se negó. Vende su casa y se instala en la editorial. Dos semanas más tarde, Voltaire envió manuscritos a Louis, pidiéndole publicar con él. Los libros se vendieron tanto que Louis pronto se convirtió en uno de los editores más populares de su época.

A MAN WITH WILL

Louis was one of those men who believed in free thinking and wasn't interested in people telling him what to do. He believed all men had the right to choose whoever they wanted to believe in, and this led him into trouble a lot of times. He was always quick to tell people off and mention how stupid he thought everyone was. Voltaire and Rousseau wrote some of his favorite books and he couldn't have a simple conversation without mentioning their names. This was the time when most publishers published books that promoted science and reason, so it wasn't surprising that he loved these books since the writers were popular. However, his obsession was becoming increasingly weird and people around him could no longer converse with him properly. He seemed unstable and he was always saying things that seemed unreasonable.

Tired of the criticism from everyone around, Louis decided to open a small publishing house so he could help bring people who wrote things he loved to a wider audience. He used all his savings and took loans to begin this publishing firm that everyone had advised against. In the first month, he searched for writers, philosophers and scientists who he could publish and found none. He sent news out to associations but no one was willing to trust his small firm. Dejected, he shut down the firm briefly for two weeks. During this time, he wrote down the names of some of the people he wanted to work with and sent letters to them, requesting their manuscripts. He opened the firm again and put out notes but got nothing. People began to insult his business logic and they reminded him of the times he called them stupid. In a bid to prove them wrong, Louis collected manuscripts about things he wasn't interested in, and published them. None of the books sold more than five pieces each and even Louis couldn't read them. He kept on sending the letters to the people whose manuscripts he wanted regardless.

After the third month Louis opened, the creditors began to disturb him. They visited his home and threatened to arrest him if he didn't pay up immediately. People advised him to sell the publishing house to raise the money needed but he refused. Instead, he sold his home and began to live in the publishing house. Two weeks later, Voltaire sent manuscripts to Louis, asking to publish with him. The books sold so much that Louis soon became one of the most popular publishers of their time.

Vocabulary

Razón	Reason
Nombres	Numbers
Conversación	Conversation
Libros	Books
Problemas	Problems
Promovido	Promoted
Interesado	Interested
Ciencia	Science
Simple	Simple
Raro	Weird
Inestable	Unstable

Vocabulary Questions

¿Qué le interesaba a Louis? What was Louis interested in?

¿Por qué criticaban a Luis? Why did people criticize Louis?

¿Cómo respondía Louis a las críticas? How did Louis respond to criticism?

Historical Note

The Age of Enlightenment was an intellectual movement that saw the rise of thinkers like Voltaire, Rousseau, and Montesquieu. It promoted reason, science, and individual rights. This period saw the publication of influential works by philosophers.

ÓDIO AMOROSO

Marco siempre había sido amigo de Napoleón Bonaparte. Se conocieron en Córcega y estuvieron más unidos que hermanos. Fue una de las personas que animó a Napoleón a que luchara hasta convertirse en el gobernante de Francia. Estaban tan unidos que a veces la gente se preguntaba si había algo más en su amistad. Aunque Napoleón nunca habló mucho de Marco, sus acciones demostraban que se preocupaba mucho por él.

Aunque a Marco no le interesaba la milicia, se alistó en el ejército de Napoleón para poder apoyar a su amigo en los momentos importantes. Sin embargo, Marcus era un hombre frágil, tenía epilepsia y siempre sufría ataques en el momento menos oportuno. No estaba en condiciones de formar parte del ejército de Napoleón, pero éste nunca se quejó, una acción que hizo creer a la gente que Napoleón se preocupaba por él. Aunque su amistad parecía genial por fuera, a Marco había empezado a disgustarle secretamente Napoleón por sus logros. Mientras que Napoleón había ascendido como general militar, Marco era un pequeño comerciante que acababa de alistarse en el ejército. Esta antipatía creció con el tiempo y cuando Napoleón intentó dominar Europa, la antipatía de Marco se había convertido en odio total y ya no podía ocultar sus sentimientos hacia Napoleón.

Ahora, Marco se había vuelto muy inseguro de sí mismo. Su odio le cegaba y ya no podía pensar con claridad, así que habló con algunas personas que le aconsejaron que hablara con Napoleón y arreglara las cosas. Siguiendo el consejo, llamó a Napoleón una de las noches de las Guerras Napoleónicas y le comentó algunas de las cosas que le preocupaban. Napoleón se sorprendió de todo, pero no pudo quedarse a hablar porque las guerras eran más urgentes, así que prometió tratar las cosas más adelante. Esto enfadó aún más a Marco, que decidió alejarse. Creía que Napoleón ya no se preocupaba por él y ya no estaba seguro de querer permanecer en la misma ciudad con él. Se llevó a su familia y se mudó a una de las ciudades más pequeñas.

Cuando Napoleón se enteró, se sintió desolado y envió soldados para traerlos de vuelta. Sin embargo, cuando Marco se negó a seguir a los soldados, éstos lo mataron por error. Cuando Napoleón se enteró, mató él mismo a todos los soldados y se puso de luto durante días en medio de la guerra.

LOVELY HATE

Marcus had always been a friend of Napoleon Bonaparte. They knew each other in Corsica and stayed closer than brothers. He was one of the people who encouraged Napoleon that he could fight his way to becoming the ruler of France. They were so close that people sometimes wondered if there was something more to their friendship. While Napoleon never really spoke much of Marcus, his actions showed that he cared so much about the man.

Although Marcus wasn't interested in the military, he joined Napoleon's army so he could support his friend right when it mattered. However, Marcus was a fragile man, he had epilepsy and would always have seizures at the wrong time. He was not fit to be a part of Napoleon's army but Napoleon never complained, an action that made people believe that Napoleon cared for him. While their friendship looked great on the outside, Marcus had begun to secretly dislike Napoleon for his achievements. While Napoleon had risen in the ranks as a military general, Marcus was a petty trader who had just joined the army. This dislike grew over time and by the time Napoleon attempted to dominate Europe, Marcus's dislike had grown into full-blown hate and he could no longer hide his feelings for Napoleon.

Now, Marcus had become so unsure of himself. His hate was blinding him and he could no longer think straight, so he spoke to a few people who advised him to talk to Napoleon and settle things. Taking the advice, he called Napoleon on one of the nights during the Napoleon Wars and discussed some of the things bothering him. Napoleon was surprised at everything but couldn't stay to talk since the wars were more pressing, so he promised to address things at a later date. This further angered Marcus and he decided to move away. He believed that Napoleon no longer cared about him and he was no longer sure he wanted to stay in the same city with him. He took his family with him and moved to one of the smaller towns.

When Napoleon heard, he was devastated and sent soldiers to bring them back. However, when Marcus refused to follow the soldiers back, they mistakenly killed him. When Napoleon heard the news, he killed all the soldiers himself and went into mourning for days amidst the war.

Vocabulary

Soldado	Soldier
Promesa	Promise
Amigo	Friend
Guerra	War
Más cerca	Closer
Ciudad	City
Cosas	Things
Noticias	News
Hermano	Brother
Mismo	Mesmo
En medio de	Amidst
Rechazado	Refused

Comprehension Questions

¿Cuál era la relación entre Napoleón y Marco? What was the relationship between Napoleon and Marcus?

¿Por qué empezó a caerle mal a Napoleón su amigo? Why did Napoleon start to dislike his friend?

¿Por qué se marchó Marco? Why did Marcus move away?

Historical Note

The French revolution was marked by the overthrow of the monarchy, the Reign of Terror, and the rise of Napoleon Bonaparte. Napoleon's conquests and conflicts with various European powers, including the Battle of Waterloo, involved figures like Arthur Wellesley, Duke of Wellington, and various European monarchs. Spanning several conflicts, including battles like Austerlitz, Trafalgar, and Waterloo, these wars involved Napoleon's conquests and his ultimate defeat.

DESPUÉS DE

Tras la muerte de Marco, Napoleón se afligió volviendo a la guerra. En ese momento, los franceses estaban en guerra con España y Portugal y pretendían controlar tanto España como Portugal. Inicialmente, Napoleón había pensado en Marco como la persona adecuada para gobernar España y Portugal, pero con la muerte de Marco, decidió que su hermano José era la persona adecuada y lo colocó en el trono español.

Ahora, José tenía un amigo, César, que conocía los rumores de que Marco era la persona adecuada para el puesto. César nunca se preocupó por Napoleón, así que se apresuró a contarle a José los rumores. Temeroso de que Napoleón pudiera decidir que el joven hijo de Marco era más adecuado para el trono, José envió a algunos de sus soldados a casa de Marco. Los soldados llevaron a Eva, la mujer de Marco, y a su hijo, Luca, ante José por la noche. Cuando José vio que el niño era más inteligente que su edad, decidió matarlo en secreto. Envió a buscar los mejores venenos que no pudieran rastrearse fácilmente y unos días después, el niño murió sin causa conocida.

Joseph se acercó más a Eve tras la muerte de su hijo para asegurarse de que no lo viera como sospechoso. Pero, Eve sabía que algo iba mal y que no era el destino el causante de que su hijo muriera a los pocos días de mudarse, así que espió a Joseph mientras él hacía todo lo posible para que se sintiera bienvenida en su espacio.

Pronto se presentó la oportunidad adecuada cuando César visitó a José. José organizó una pequeña fiesta para César para celebrar que sus planes funcionaban, hablaron de todo, sin darse cuenta de que Eva estaba escuchando debido al alcohol. Eva pudo descubrir la razón exacta de la muerte de su hijo y pronto planeó lo mismo para José y César. En su ira, envenenó a César inmediatamente y por la mañana ya estaba muerto, lo que obligó a José a aumentar el número de soldados que lo guiaban. José avisó a Napoleón de la muerte de César, creyendo que había sido uno de sus enemigos, pero Napoleón estaba demasiado ocupado con las guerras como para preocuparse por una muerte tonta. Muy pronto, José encontró consuelo en la compañía de Eva y le contaba todo mientras ella lo saboteaba con la información que obtenía. Eva siguió saboteando a José hasta el final, acción que contribuyó a la derrota final de Napoleón.

AFTER

After Marcus's death, Napoleon grieved by going back to war. At this time, the French were at war with Spain and Portugal and were seeking to control both Spain and Portugal. Initially, Napoleon had thought of Marcus as the right person to rule over Spain and Portugal, but with Marcus's death, he decided that his brother, Joseph was the right person and placed him on the Spanish throne.

Now, Joseph had a friend, Caesar who knew about the rumors that Marcus was the right person for the position. Caesar never really cared about Napoleon so he was quick to tell Joseph about the rumors. Afraid that Napoleon could decide that Marcus's young son was a better fit for the throne, Joseph sent a few of his soldiers to Marcus's home. The soldiers brought Eve, Marcus's wife and his son, Luca to Joseph in the night. When Joseph saw that the child was smarter than his age, he decided to kill the child in secret. He sent for the best poisons that couldn't be traced easily and a few days later, the boy died without a known cause.

Joseph became closer to Eve after her son's death to ensure that she didn't see him as a suspect. But, Eve knew something was wrong and it wasn't fate that caused her child to die a few days after she moved, so she spied on Joseph while he tried his best to make her feel welcome in his space.

Soon, the right opportunity presented itself when Caesar visited Joseph. Joseph threw a small party for Caesar to celebrate their plans working out, they talked about everything, without realizing that Eve was listening due to the alcohol. Eve was able to discover the exact reason her son died and she soon planned the same thing for Joseph and Caesar. In her anger, she poisoned Caesar immediately and he was dead by morning, forcing Joseph to increase the number of soldiers guiding him. Joseph reached out to Napoleon about Caesar's death, believing that it was from one of their enemies but Napoleon was too caught up in the wars to bother about a silly death. Soon enough, Joseph found comfort in Eve's company and he would tell her about everything while she sabotaged him with the information she got. Eva continued to sabotage Joseph until the very end, an action that contributed to Napoleon's eventual defeat.

Vocabulary

Duelo	Grief
Controlar	Control
Pronto	Soon
Celebrar	Celebrate
Pequeño	Small
Acción	Action
Aumentar	Increase
Lanzar	Threw
Exacto	Exact
Número	Number
Partido	Party
Sabotaje	Sabotage
Empresa	Company
Molestar	Bother

Comprehension Questions

¿Qué países estaban en guerra? What countries were at war?

¿Cómo se enteró Eva de los planes de César y José? How did Eve find out Caesar and Joseph's plans?

¿Cómo saboteó Eva a José? How did Eve sabotage Joseph?

Historical Note

Spain's alliance with France under Napoleon led to the Peninsular War, involving figures like Joseph Bonaparte and the Spanish guerrilla leaders. The alliance between Spain and France led to Napoleon's invasion, the Peninsular War, and the subsequent Spanish revolt against French occupation.

LA VOZ DE LA MUERTE

Rena era uno de los hombres de Napoleón que luchó con él durante la mayor parte de la guerra de Napoleón. Había estado allí durante la vida de Marco y luchó en las batallas inmediatamente posteriores. Aunque era un hombre muy carismático, no le interesaba tanto la guerra. Sólo estaba allí para cumplir el último deseo de su madre, que era apoyar a Napoleón, quien la había salvado cuando era más joven. Así pues, Rena se alistó poco después en el ejército y desde entonces fue leal a Napoleón. Fue uno de los hombres que aconsejó a Marcus que abandonara la capital cuando su odio le estaba llevando fuera de control.

Aunque Rena era un buen soldado, rara vez luchaba y, cuando lo hacía, nunca lo hacía durante mucho tiempo. Prefería cantar a los soldados mientras descansaban. Así, cada vez que luchaban, cantaba para calmarlos. También iba a las ciudades y cantaba para las mujeres que lloraban a sus maridos y para los niños que lloraban a sus madres. Decía a la gente que le encantaba cantar porque sólo las canciones le hacían feliz tras la muerte de su madre. Pronto se hizo famoso como la voz de la muerte. Se extendió el rumor de que la gente moría allí donde se oía su voz y la gente empezó a temerla. Sin embargo, Rena siguió cantando aunque su canto causara terror entre la gente. La mayoría de los soldados le aconsejaron que dejara de cantar, pero él se mantuvo firme y empezó a adentrarse en el bosque para cantar a los animales.

Un día, mientras cantaba en el bosque, oyó un sonido que le recordó a su madre. Curioso, siguió el sonido hasta llegar a un pequeño claro en lo profundo del bosque. Allí vio al pájaro y se lo llevó con él. Pero el pájaro dejó de cantar inmediatamente después de salir del bosque. Al día siguiente, se llevó el pájaro al bosque, pero al adentrarse en él, el pájaro empezó a cantar de nuevo. Volvió a llevárselo a casa y ocurrió lo mismo: el pájaro se negó a cantar. Alimentó al pájaro, pero nada cambió, así que recogió su ropa y se llevó al pájaro de vuelta a una parte más profunda del bosque. Instaló una cabaña y vivió en el bosque durante toda la guerra.

Cuando se enteró de la derrota de Napoleón en la batalla de Waterloo, regresó con el pájaro y cantó para Napoleón durante días antes de retirarse al bosque con su pájaro. La gente dice que oye su voz cada vez que entra en un bosque.

THE VOICE OF DEATH

Rena was one of Napoleon's men who fought with him during most of Napoleon's war. He had been there during Marcus's life and fought in the battles immediately after. Although he was a very charismatic man, he was not so interested in the war. He was just there to fulfill his mother's dying wish which was to support Napoleon who had saved her when she was younger. So, Rena joined the army soon after and since then, he had been loyal to Napoleon. He was one of the men who advised Marcus to leave the capital when his hate was driving him out of control.

Although Rena was a good soldier, he rarely fought and when he did, he never fought for long periods. He preferred to sing to the soldiers while they rested. So, every time they fought, he would sing to calm them down. He would also go into the towns and sing for the women grieving their husbands and children grieving their mothers. He would tell people that he loved to sing because only songs made him happy after his mother's death. Soon, he gained fame as the voice of death. Rumors spread that people died wherever his voice was heard and people began to dread his voice. Yet, Rena continued singing even as his singing caused terror among people. Most of the soldiers advised him to stop singing but he remained adamant and began to go into the forest to sing to the animals.

One day, while singing in the forest, he heard a sound that reminded him of his mother. Curious, he traced the sound until he reached a small clearing deep in the forest. There, he saw the bird and took it with him. But, the bird stopped singing immediately after they left the forest. The next day, he took the bird to the forest but as he moved deeper into the forest, the bird began to sing again. He took the bird home with him again and the same thing happened: the bird refused to sing. He fed the bird yet nothing changed so he packed his clothes and led the bird back to a deeper part of the forest. He set up a hut and lived in the forest all through the war.

When he heard of Napoleon's defeat at the Battle of Waterloo, he went back with the bird and sang for Napoleon for days before retreating into the forest with his bird. People say they hear his voice whenever they enter a forest.

Vocabulary

Buena	Good
Rara vez	Rarely
Nada	Nothing
Derrota	Defeat
Rastreado	Traced
Bosque	Forest
Ropa	Clothes
Pájaro	Bird
Batalla	Battle
Recordado	Reminded
Canta	Sing
Preferido	Prefered
Día	Day
Inmediatamente	Immediately
Sonido	Sound

Comprehension Questions

¿Por qué estaba Rena en el ejército? Why was Rena in the army?

¿Qué le gustaba hacer a Rena? What did Rena love doing?

¿Por qué a la gente le aterrorizaba que Rena cantara? Why were people terrified of Rena's singing?

Historical Note

The defeat of Napoleon led to his exile and the restoration of European monarchies, including the Congress of Vienna. He was exiled to the remote island of Saint Helena in the South Atlantic, where he spent the remainder of his life until his death in 1821.

NIÑO OBSTINADO

Hace años, muchos países estaban bajo dominio español y personas como Simón Bolívar hicieron mucho para que varios países sudamericanos se libraran de los españoles. Fue durante estas batallas y revueltas cuando Emily nació en España. El nacimiento de Emily fue un milagro ya que sus padres habían buscado un hijo durante 10 años antes del nacimiento de Emily, por lo que era normal que la protegieran de las duras costumbres del mundo. Los vecinos y todos los demás se esforzaron para que Emily tuviera una buena vida. Emily era el milagro de todos y todos estaban contentos de criarla bien.

Pronto, Emily empezó a aprovecharse del amor de todos. Robaba cosas y, cuando la pillaban, lloraba durante horas hasta que la dejaban marchar sin castigarla. Vee, la madre de Emily, temerosa de disgustarla, no decía nada y la dejaba marchar. Con el tiempo, la gente de su entorno empezó a quejarse de la grosería de Emily con todo el mundo y cada vez que hablaban, Vee les decía que la dejaran en paz. No pasó mucho tiempo hasta que todos ignoraron a Emily y ordenaron a sus hijos que no volvieran a jugar con ella. Los amigos de Emily dejaron de visitarla y, como a ella tampoco se le permitía hacerlo, pronto se sintió sola y enferma. Vee trató a Emily con todo lo que sabía, pero no mejoraba. Llevó a Emily al médico, pero nada cambió. Decidió visitar a sus vecinos y rogarles que visitaran a Emily. Después de la visita, los niños y sus padres se acercaron a hablar con Emily y pronto se puso bien. Sin embargo, Emily no había dejado de ser maleducada y mezquina con todo el mundo, así que los niños acabaron dejando de visitarla en cuanto se puso bien.

Dos días después, la abuela de Emily la visitó y enseguida se dio cuenta de que estaba maleducada. Habló con Vee y ambas decidieron que Emily necesitaba aprender algunas lecciones. Vee habló con su madre sobre el miedo que le daba tocar a Emily y acordaron corregirla con suavidad salvo en casos extremos. Así que, todas las noches, la abuela de Emily le contaba cuentos folclóricos sobre niños testarudos, creando así el miedo en la mente de Emily. Emily no tardó en darse cuenta de que había perdido a todos sus amigos y que podía ser castigada severamente por Dios si se portaba mal. Pidió a su abuela que la siguiera hasta los vecinos, se disculpó con todos y recuperó a sus amigos.

OBSTINATE CHILD

Years ago, a lot of countries were under Spanish rule and people like Simón Bolívar did a lot to ensure that various South American countries were free from the Spanish. It was during these battles and revolts that Emily was born in Spain. Emily's birth was a miracle as her parents had sought a child for 10 years before Emily's birth, so it was only normal for them to shield her from the harsh ways of the world. The neighbors and everyone around were dedicated to ensuring that Emily lived a good life. Emily was everyone's miracle and they were all happy to raise her well.

Soon, Emily began to use the love from everyone. She would steal things and when she was caught, she would cry for hours until they let her go without punishment. Afraid of upsetting her, Emily's mother, Vee would say nothing and allow her to go. Over time, people around them began to complain about Emily's rudeness to everyone around and each time they spoke, Vee would tell them to leave her alone. It wasn't long before everyone ignored Emily and instructed their children to never play with her again. Emily's friends stopped visiting her and since she wasn't allowed to visit them as well, she soon became lonely and sick. Vee treated Emily with everything she knew yet she wasn't getting any better. She took Emily to the doctor yet nothing changed. She decided to visit her neighbors and beg them to visit Emily. After the visit, the children and their parents came around and spoke to Emily and she soon became well. However, Emily had not stopped being rude and petty to everyone so the children eventually stopped visiting immediately she was fine.

Two days later, Emily's grandmother visited and quickly noticed that she was ill-mannered. So, she spoke to Vee and they both decided that Emily needed to learn some lessons. Vee talked to her mother about how she was too afraid to touch Emily and they agreed to correct her gently except in extreme cases. So, every night, Emily's grandmother would tell folklore about stubborn children, thereby creating fear in Emily's mind. Emily soon realized that she had lost all her friends and she could be punished severely by God if she misbehaved. She asked her grandmother to follow her to the neighbors, apologized to everyone and gained her friends back.

Vocabulary

Terco	Stubborn
Lección	Lessons
Visitado	Visited
Abuela	Grandmother
Suavemente	Gently
Seguir	Follow
Castigado	Punished
Vecinos	Neighbors
Habló	Spoke
Extremar	Extreme
Pedir disculpas	Apologize
Aprender	Learn
Folklore	Folklore
Corregir	Correct

Vocabulary Questions

¿Qué hizo especial el nacimiento de Emily? What made Emily's birth special?

¿Por qué los amigos de Emily dejaron de visitarla? Why did Emily's friends stop visiting her?

¿Cómo corrigió su comportamiento la abuela de Emily? How did Emily's grandmother correct her behavior?

Historical Notes

Various revolts and battles led to the independence of countries in South America from Spanish rule, spearheaded by leaders like Bolívar and San Martín.

CEGADO POR EL AMOR

Jude entró en palacio con la cabeza bien alta para ver a su tío, Jacobo II, el rey de Inglaterra. Aunque no todo iba bien, se había prometido a sí mismo que iba a estar siempre alegre hasta el final. Las cosas no iban muy bien, pero él creía firmemente que podrían arreglarse y que su tío permanecería en el trono durante mucho tiempo. La mayoría de la población inglesa de la época estaba cansada de la monarquía y dispuesta a abrazar el sistema monárquico parlamentario. Querían ser liberales y ya había planes para librar a Inglaterra del monarca, pero Jude tenía esperanzas. Creía que la familia merecía estar ahí en el poder, como todas las demás familias que habían gobernado a lo largo del tiempo. Así que iba a hacer todo lo que estuviera en su mano para apoyar a su tío.

Al entrar en la habitación de James, Jude no se sorprendió al ver que estaba triste e inseguro por todo lo que estaba pasando, aunque no lo pareciera a la gente de alrededor. Jude habló de algunas de las formas en que podían influir en las cosas pero James ya no sabía si podía creer las palabras de Jude. Jude parecía demasiado positivo y él sólo quería la verdad, así que le pidió a Jude que se fuera para poder pensar bien.

Con la promesa de que volvería al día siguiente, Jude se marchó y fue a reunirse con algunas personas para que pudieran influir en las cosas y asegurarse de que James no fuera derrocado. Al día siguiente, Jude volvió a Palacio, pero fue expulsado de nuevo.

Temió que su tío ya no le necesitara y acudió a su madre. Le suplicó que hablara con James, pero ella no le hizo caso. Ella ya estaba cansada de su obsesión con el rey, sobre todo con todo lo que estaba pasando. Le aconsejó que se olvidara de intentar detener todo el proceso y que se centrara en lo que podían hacer a pesar de lo que estaba pasando. Jude se marchó enfadado de su casa mientras insistía en que el trono era legítimamente de su tío y nadie podía arrebatárselo. Se reunió con sus amigos e intentó convencerles de que le ayudaran para que Jaime pudiera seguir en el trono, pero ninguno de ellos estaba dispuesto a ayudar. Al final, Jaime fue derrocado y se instauró una monarquía constitucional. Jude se puso en contacto con Jaime y, al no obtener respuesta, se suicidó. En su entierro, su madre repitió a todo el mundo que amaba a su tío más que a sí mismo y que ese amor le mató.

BLINDED BY LOVE

Jude walked into the palace, his head high up as he made to see his uncle, James II, the king of England. Although everything wasn't fine, he had promised himself that he was always going to be cheerful until the very end. Things weren't going so well, but he believed strongly that they could work things out and that his uncle would stay on the throne for a very long time. Most of the people in England at the time were tired of the monarchy and ready to embrace the parliamentary system of monarchy. They wanted to be liberal and plans were already underway to rid England of the monarch but Jude was hopeful. He believed that the family deserved to be there in power, just like every other family that had ruled over time. So, he was going to do everything in his power to support his uncle.

On entering James' chambers, Jude wasn't surprised to see that he was sad and unsure about everything going on although he didn't seem that way to people around. Jude talked about some of the ways they could influence things but James no longer knew if he could believe Jude's words. Jude seemed too positive and he just wanted the truth, so he asked Jude to leave so he could think well.

With the promise that he would be back the next day, Jude left and went on to meet a few people so they could influence things and ensure James wasn't overthrown. The next day, Jude went back to the Palace but was sent away again.

He became afraid that his uncle no longer needed him and went to his mother. He begged her to speak to James but she didn't listen. She was already tired of his obsession with the king, especially with everything that was going on. She advised him to forget about trying to stop the whole process and just focus on what they could do regardless of what was happening. Jude left her place in anger while insisting that the throne was rightfully his uncle's and no one could take it away. He met with his friends and tried to convince them to help him so James could remain on the throne but none of them was willing to help. Ultimately, James was overthrown and a constitutional monarchy was established. Jude reached out to James and when he got no response, he committed suicide. At his burial, his mother repeatedly told everyone that he loved his uncle more than himself and that love killed him.

Vocabulary

Miedo	Afraid
Madre	Mother
Trono	Throne
Suicidio	Suicide
Todos	Everyone
Proceso	Process
Influir	Influence
Garantizar	Ensure
Palacio	Palace
Convencer	Convince
Permanecer	Remain
Responder	Response
Ira	Anger
Ayuda	Help

Comprehension Questions

¿Cuál era la preocupación de Jude? What was Jude's concern?

¿Cómo intentó influir Judas? How did Jude try to influence things?

¿Qué le ocurrió al final a Santiago? What happened to James in the end?

Historical Note

The Glorious Revolution in England symbolizes the shift of power from the monarchy to Parliament, laying the groundwork for constitutional monarchy and the rise of liberalism. James II was overthrown during this period.

LA NOCHE CON EL GENERAL

Matías temblaba de frío mientras recorría el camino que conducía a la tienda del general Francisco Franko. Era un soldado del ejército de Franko y habían estado luchando contra la República bajo el mando del general. La mayoría de ellos creían que la República española no debía existir y se había convertido en una lucha de republicanos contra nacionalistas. La lucha se estaba volviendo poco a poco demasiado sangrienta y Matthias ya no estaba seguro de por qué luchaban. Por mucho que creyera que luchaban por los nacionalistas, seguía preguntándose si las matanzas merecían la pena y ya no tenía una respuesta sencilla como antes. Tenían poco tiempo para dormir y a él le costaba conciliar el sueño en esas horas. Cuando finalmente encontraba el sueño, éste se llenaba con los rostros de algunas de las personas que habían matado durante la guerra. Ahora, necesitaba reunirse con Franko para que le dijera algunas palabras que le ayudaran a sentirse mejor. Sabía que Franko no era un predicador ni una esperanza, pero creía que la motivación del general también podría hacer algo por él.

Aunque hacía frío, Matthias no temblaba de frío, estaba acostumbrado al clima ya que habían luchado en peores condiciones. Temblaba por el miedo al general. No estaba seguro de cómo lo recibiría el general y no sabía si su decisión de buscarlo era buena.

El general estaba en medio de otros dos hombres cuando Matías llegó y, sorprendentemente, estaban allí para quejarse de lo mismo. Habían matado tanto que ya no encontraban bien el sueño y el general les hablaba con calma, como nunca había visto Matías. Franko les recordó las razones por las que estalló la guerra en primer lugar y cómo se necesitaban mutuamente para ganar. Les recordó sus creencias y les preguntó si querían que la República Española siguiera existiendo. Las palabras animaron a los hombres y, cuando llegaron a sus tiendas, se lo contaron a los demás hasta que se corrió la voz entre los hombres y todos estuvieron dispuestos a seguir luchando por lo que creían.

Muy pronto, los republicanos se rindieron a las fuerzas nacionalistas. Aunque el general pasó a convertirse en un gobernante dictador, Matthias nunca olvidaría aquella noche en la que el general Franko agitó a los hombres.

THE NIGHT WITH THE GENERAL

Matthias shivered against the cold as he walked the pathway that led to General Francisco Franko's tent. He was a soldier in Franko's army and they had been fighting the Republic under the general. Most of them believed that the Spanish Republic wasn't supposed to be and it had turned into a Republican versus Nationalists fight. The fight was gradually becoming too bloody and Matthias was no longer sure what they were fighting for. As much as he believed that they were fighting for Nationalists, he kept wondering if the killings were worth it and he didn't have a simple answer like he used to. They had little time to sleep and he was finding it difficult to sleep in those hours. When he eventually found sleep, it would be filled with the faces of some of the people they had killed during the war. Now, he needed to meet with Franko just to get some words that would help him feel better. He knew Franko was no preacher or hope but he believed that the general's motivation could do something for him as well.

Although it was cold, Matthias wasn't shivering from the cold, he was used to the weather as they had fought in worse conditions. He was shivering from the fear of the general. He wasn't sure about how the general would receive him and he didn't know if his decision to seek him out was a good one.

The general was in the midst of two of the other men when Matthias got there and surprisingly, they were there to complain about the same thing. They had killed so much that they no longer found sleep as well and the general was talking to them calmly, unlike anything Matthias had ever seen. Franko reminded them of the reasons the war broke out in the first place and how they needed each other to win. He reminded them of their beliefs and asked each of them if they wanted the Spanish Republic to continue to exist. The words encouraged the men and when they got to their tents, they told the others until the word spread amongst the men and they were all ready to keep fighting for what they believed.

Soon enough, the republicans surrendered to the nationalist forces. Although the general went on to become a dictator ruler, Matthias would never forget that night when General Franko stirred up the men.

Vocabulary

Difundir	Spread
Frío	Cold
Dictador	Dictator
Tiendas	Tents
Decisión	Decision
Quejarse	Complain
Fuerzas	Forces
A diferencia de	Unlike
Dormir	Sleep
Necesario	Needed
Cualquier cosa	Anything
Con calma	Calmly
Miedo	Fear
Recibir	Receive

Comprehension Questions

¿A qué se dedicaba Mathias? What was Mathias occupation?

¿Por qué temblaba Mathias? Why did Mathias shiver?

¿Qué cosas les dijo Franko a los soldados? What things did Franko tell the soldiers?

Historical Notes

The Second Spanish Republic emerged in the 1930s, leading to the Spanish Civil War between Republicans and Nationalists led by Franco. The establishment of the Second Spanish Republic led to political tensions, eventually erupting into the Spanish Civil War between Republicans and Nationalists, resulting in Franco's rise to power.

HILOS DE AMISTAD

Aunque Franko fue un gobernante famoso en España, como cualquier otro hombre, cedió a la enfermedad de Parkinson en la vejez y Juan Carlos se convirtió en el jefe de Estado en funciones cada vez que Franko estaba demasiado enfermo. Franko se negó a que su salud tomara las riendas y cada vez que se encontraba mejor, volvía a asumir su papel. Pero, pronto cayó en coma y murió de un ataque al corazón en 1975 a los 82 años. Juan Carlos no tardó en convertirse en Jefe del Estado y su viejo amigo Joel se alegró mucho de la noticia. A Joel nunca le gustó Franko y creía que estaba impidiendo que Juan se convirtiera en Jefe de Estado cuando era obvio que ya no estaba en condiciones. Aunque Franko había declarado a Juan su sucesor 6 años antes de su muerte, Joel no estaba convencido de Franko.

Nada más conocer la noticia de la muerte de Franko, Joel organizó una fiesta a pesar de que el país estaba de luto. Invitó a todos a comer y beber y, como era amigo de Juan, nadie se lo impidió.

No pasó mucho tiempo hasta que Juan y Joel empezaron a tener problemas entre ellos. Debido a las acciones de Joel, se había extendido el rumor de que Juan debía tener algo que ver con la muerte de Franko y como eso no era cierto, Juan amonestó a Joel. Esto enfureció a Joel porque esperaba el apoyo de Juan y él no veía nada malo en sus acciones y pronto dejó de enviar cartas a Juan.

Cuando las cartas de Joel a Juan dejaron de llegar, Juan se sintió aliviado y se centró en la transición a la democracia. Cuando Joel se dio cuenta de que sus acciones no habían conmovido en absoluto a Juan, envió otra carta, expresando su enfado. Juan envió una carta en respuesta, en la que le decía que se calmara y dejara de causar problemas. Sorprendido, Joel envía otra carta en la que le dice a Juan que su amistad ha terminado.

Joel emigró a otro país con su familia después de enviar la carta. No podía seguir bajo el dominio de Juan. El tiempo fuera de España ayudó a Joel a pensar detenidamente sobre su papel en la ruptura y pronto se dio cuenta de que había ignorado el efecto de sus acciones. Volvió a España, se reunió con Juan y discutieron. Aclararon las cosas y Joel se dio cuenta de que Juan estaba en una posición en la que ya no podía tolerar su comportamiento para evitar un alboroto. Hasta la abdicación de Juan, siguieron siendo buenos amigos.

Se trata de un relato de ficción, adaptado de la vida del rey Juan Carlos I, que reinó como rey de España entre 1975 y 2014.

STRINGS OF FRIENDSHIP

Although Franko was a famous ruler in Spain, just like every other man, he gave in to Parkinson's disease in old age and Juan Carlos became the acting head of state whenever Franko was too sick. Franko refused to allow his health to take charge and each time he was better, he would assume his role back. But, he soon fell into a coma and died of a heart attack in 1975 at 82 years. Juan Carlos soon became the head of state and his old friend, Joel was overjoyed at the news. Joel never really liked Franko and believed he was stopping Juan from becoming head of state when it was obvious he was no longer fit. Although Franko had declared Juan as his successor 6 years before his death, Joel wasn't convinced about Franko.

Immediately Joel heard the news of Franko's death, he threw a party although the country was mourning. He invited everyone to eat and drink and because he was friends with Juan, nobody stopped him.

It wasn't long until Juan and Joel began to have problems between themselves. Due to Joel's actions, rumors had spread that Juan must have had something to do with Franko's death and since that wasn't true, Juan cautioned Joel. This angered Joel because he expected support from Juan and he didn't see anything wrong with his actions and he soon stopped sending letters to Juan.

When the letters from Joel to Juan stopped coming in, Juan was relieved and he focused on transitioning to democracy. When Joel found out that his actions had not stirred Juan at all, he sent another letter, expressing his anger. Juan sent a letter in response, where he told him to calm down and stop causing trouble. Surprised, Joel sent another letter in which he told Juan that their friendship was over.

Joel migrated to another country with his family after sending the letter. He couldn't stay under Juan's rule. The time away from Spain helped Joel to think carefully about his role in their breakup and he soon realized that he had been ignorant about the effect of his actions. He moved back to Spain, met up with Juan and they discussed. They cleared up things and Joel realized that Juan was in a position where he could no longer tolerate his behavior to prevent an uproar. Until Juan's abdication, they remained good friends.

This is a fictional tale, adapted from the life of King Juan Carlos I who reigned as king of Spain between 1975 and 2014.

Vocabulary

Equivocado	Wrong
Problemas	Problems
Verdadero	True
Alboroto	Uproar
Papel	Role
Otro	Another
Carta	Letter
Ignorante	Ignorant
Hasta	Until
Lejos	Away

Comprehension Questions

¿Qué hizo Joel durante su ausencia? What did Joel do in his time away?

¿Qué dijo Joel en su última carta a Juan? What did Joel say in his last letter to Juan?

¿Qué le ocurrió al anterior gobernante, Franko? What happened to the previous ruler, Franko?

Historical Notes

After Franco's death, Spain transitioned to democracy. Key figures include King Juan Carlos I, who played a pivotal role in the transition, and modern political figures like José Luis Rodríguez Zapatero and Mariano Rajoy. Spain's transition to democracy after Franco's death, marked by a new constitution, and its subsequent economic, social, and political developments till present times.

Conclusion

Learning the basics of any language is difficult, and the Spanish language can feel daunting for many newcomers. With that being said, if you were able to finish all of the lessons in this book, you have built a solid foundation in Spanish.

However, learning a language is a long process that rewards consistency. Even just listening and watching Spanish shows for 30 minutes a day can go a long way in improving your Spanish skills. We sincerely hope that you continue your Spanish language journey with the foundation you have built up and reach your goals, whether that be to understand the basics or speak like a native.

Thank you for choosing our book along your path to Spanish mastery and we hope that you obtained a lot of useful information! If you have any questions, comments, or even suggestions we would love to hear from you by email at Contact@worldwidenomadbooks.com. We greatly appreciate the feedback and this allows us to improve our books and provide the best language learning experience we can.

Thank you,

Worldwide Nomad Team

Made in United States
Troutdale, OR
02/06/2024

17490595R00175